M000158620

SICILY

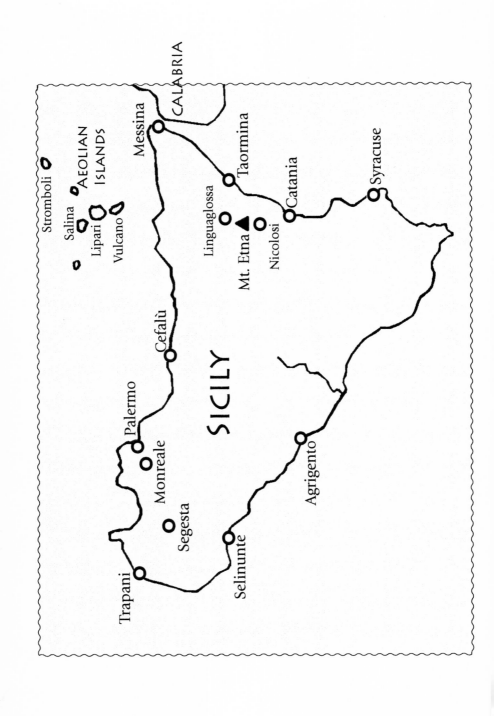

SICILY

BY

GUY DE MAUPASSANT

TRANSLATED AND EDITED
BY ROBERT W. BERGER

ITALICA PRESS
NEW YORK
2007

Translation Copyright © 2007 by Robert W. Berger

ITALICA PRESS, INC.
595 Main Street, Suite 605
New York, New York 10044

All rights reserved. No part of this publication may be repro-
duced, stored in a retrieval system, or transmitted, in any form
or by any means, electronic, mechanical, photocopying, record-
ing, or otherwise, without prior permission of Italica Press. For
permission to reproduce selected portions for courses, or other
uses, please contact the Press at inquiries@italicapress.com.

Library of Congress Cataloging-in-Publication Data
Maupassant, Guy de, 1850-1893.
    [Sicile. English]
    Sicily / by Guy de Maupassant ; translated and edited by Robert W.
Berger.
        p. cm. — (Italica historical travel guides)
    Summary: "An English translation of Guy de Maupassant's description
of his trip around Sicily and the neighboring islands in the Spring of 1885,
with an introduction, notes and bibliography; illustrated with nineteenth-
century engravings"--Provided by publisher.
    Includes bibliographical references and index.
    ISBN 978-1-59910-008-1 (pbk. : alk. paper)
    1. Maupassant, Guy de, 1850-1893 — Travel — Italy — Sicily. 2. Sicily
(Italy) — Description and travel. 3. Authors, French — 19th century
— Biography. I. Berger, Robert W. II. Title.
    PQ2350.S5E5 2007
    843'.8—dc22
                                                                        2007022162

Cover: The *Trinacria*, symbol of Sicily.

For a Complete List of
Italica Historical Travel Titles
Visit Our Web Site at
www.italicapress.com

ABOUT THE EDITOR

Robert W. Berger (Ph.D. in Fine Arts, Harvard University) has taught at Brandeis University (chairman, 1975–77), and has been a visiting professor at Brown University, The Pennsylvania State University, and the University of Virginia. He has published extensively on French art and architecture of the period of Louis XIV and on the history of Paris.

Also by Robert W. Berger:
Antoine Le Pautre: A French Architect of the Era of Louis XIV.
Versailles: The Château of Louis XIV.
In the Garden of the Sun King: Studies on the Park of Versailles under Louis XIV.
The Palace of the Sun: The Louvre of Louis XIV.
A Royal Passion: Louis XIV as Patron of Architecture.
Public Access to Art in Paris: A Documentary History from the Middle Ages to 1800.
In Old Paris: An Anthology of Source Descriptions, 1323–1790.
Paris: An Electronic Tour of the Old City.

Forthcoming:
(with Thomas F. Hedin), *Diplomatic Tours in the Gardens of Versailles under Louis XIV.*
Jean de La Fontaine: *Journey from Paris to the Limousin: Letters to Madame de La Fontaine (1663).*

CONTENTS

ILLUSTRATIONS

ACKNOWLEDGMENTS

I first became aware of Guy de Maupassant's account of his Sicilian travels when visiting the Palatine Chapel in Palermo. While awaiting entrance, I purchased an illustrated guide and came upon a long extract from Maupassant extolling that building. After returning from my tour of Sicily, I read his *La Sicile*, and delighted in the fact that he had visited so many of the places that my wife and I had just experienced. So in preparing this edition, I have had the pleasure of reviewing my Sicilian memories and comparing them to the great writer's impressions when he was there in 1885.

I am grateful to Michael Kaufman for his critical reading of my introduction and to my wife, Susan Robbins Berger, for accompanying me to Sicily and sharing her enthusiasm for Persephone's Island.

R.W.B.

INTRODUCTION

Guy de Maupassant (1850–93) wrote "Boule de Suif," his first short-story masterpiece, in 1880 and read it aloud before publication to a literary group that included Émile Zola, J. K. Huysmans, Henry Céard and a few others. When he finished, the group spontaneously rose to their feet in tribute. This unforgettable story about a French prostitute traveling with an assorted group of bourgeois in the midst of the Franco-Prussian War marks the maturation of a rare literary genius, whose subsequent, intense production over the next ten years was justly accorded national and international acclaim, affirming the admiration of Zola's coterie. The short stories and novels that Maupassant produced before his untimely death at the age of forty-three have earned him a secure niche in French and world literature. The present volume reveals his talent in another genre, which he occasionally took up, the travel memoir.

Maupassant was a physically active and restless man. During the 1870s, when he was in his twenties, he would go rowing on the Seine, and one of his companions reminisced in later years: "From the first days of spring Maupassant's blood boiled in his veins like sap. He thirsted for fresh air and country and found it impossible to stay in Paris." Guy, who grew up under Norman skies and later lived in the capital, once wrote to his mother: "How good it would be to live in a land where there was always sun!"

His travels to sunny climes began in 1880 (Corsica) and continued throughout the decade: 1881 (Algeria), 1885 (Italy), 1887–88 (Morocco, Algeria, Tunis), 1888–89

(Algeria once more), 1889 (second trip to Italy). Only in 1886 did he briefly venture to the north, to England, where he was escorted about by Henry James, the American-born author and critic, who was fluent in French (Maupassant spoke no English).

The Italian travels of April–May 1885, which included Sicily, immediately followed the completion of Maupassant's sensational novel *Bel-Ami* in February of that year and its appearance during the spring in serial form in the pages of the newspaper *Gil Blas* (it appeared in book form in May). By this time, the writer was enjoying great acclaim, ever since publication of "Boule de Suif" (1880) and "La Maison Tellier" (1881), his first great short stories.

Maupassant was now on a well-deserved holiday. He left for Italy with two friends, the painters Henri Gervex and Georges Legrand, and the trio followed the classical route: Venice, Florence, Rome, Naples; in the last city they were joined by the minor writer Henri Amic, another friend. Maupassant climbed Vesuvius, the painters returned to Paris for the Vernissage, and Maupassant and Amic went on together, touring southern Italy and then sailing to Palermo. But Amic is never mentioned by name in the pages of Sicily (on p. 23 there is mention of "[a] friend accompanying me," but that is all).

Upon returning to Paris in May 1885, Maupassant immediately began publishing his Sicilian travel memoirs in installments in the newspapers *Le Figaro* and *Gil Blas*; the last appeared in January of the next year. An integral publication of "La Sicile" appeared in 1886 in *La nouvelle revue* and in 1890 it was published as one chapter among several in *La vie errante (The Wandering Life)*. This includes material on Italy and North Africa, garnered from his wanderings throughout the 1880s (the first chapter, "Lassitude," has references to the Exposition Universelle of 1889 and the Tour Eiffel, completed that year). Some critics consider *La vie errante* the best of his three travel collections; the other two are *Au Soleil* (In the Sun, 1884), mostly about North Africa, and *Sur l'Eau (Afloat*, 1888), mainly about sailing on the Mediterranean.

These travel writings, although minor offshoots within Maupassant's oeuvre, are nevertheless the works of a literary genius and are unfailingly engaging and masterfully written; *Sicily* in particular deserves a wider readership, which this edition is meant to foster. For in *Sicily* we find fascinating descriptions of the island, its people and landscape, including the author's dramatic ascent of Mount Etna; extended writing on architecture and works of art; and passages revelatory of the author's personal views and inner preoccupations.

Maupassant begins his travel memoir by stating: "People are convinced in France that Sicily is an uncivilized country, difficult and even dangerous to visit." That attitude, the writer is at pains to demonstrate, does not correspond to the reality of the 1880s, but there were good reasons for tourists' apprehensions. Sicily was a backward agricultural country, virtually untouched by the Industrial Revolution and structured along feudal lines. Maupassant had the luxury of traveling by railroad, which allowed him to range over the island from west to east, but the first Sicilian railroads were not built until 1860, when the island became part of the Kingdom of Italy and was no longer ruled from Naples by the Spanish Bourbons, under whose rule Sicily had stagnated. Before the railroad, travelers could only move by horse or mule along footpaths, dried-out river beds, or wretched roads, usually without bridges. Wheeled transport was thus impossible, and an official report as late as 1910 stated that many Sicilians had never seen a wheeled cart. For these reasons, much of the island was uninhabited. Accommodations for travelers, although adequate in the main cities, were primitive in the countryside. The fear of *banditti* was very real, and during and after the anti-Bourbon revolution of 1848–49, the breakdown in government allowed armed bands to seize power in villages. After 1860, gang warfare actually worsened, and a theatrical play of 1863 about life in the main prison of Palermo was called "I Mafiusi [*sic*] della Vicaria," the first association of that local dialect word to criminal behavior. Maupassant assures his readers that "[n]othing is less dangerous today than to travel through this dreaded Sicily, whether by train, by horse, or even on foot," reflecting the improved conditions for travelers in the 1880s. But concern for personal safety continued understandably to haunt the minds of visitors.

Maupassant saw a fair amount of the island. After his sojourn in Palermo and a visit to nearby Monreale, he traveled by railroad to a station in western Sicily; this served as a jumping-off point for visiting the ancient Greek sites of Segesta, Selinunte and Agrigento, which he reached apparently on horseback. Some miles due north of Agrigento he toured the sulphur mines in the region of Casteltermini. The narrative suddenly shifts to Messina and a midnight steamboat ride to the Aeolian Islands, located off the northeast coast; apparently, Maupassant had returned to Palermo and traveled by rail along the northern coast to Messina. After returning to that city by boat and taking the train south to Catania, he again went north along the eastern coast to Taormina. Back again in Catania, he sets out for the ascent of Etna, first by carriage, then by mule, finally on foot. After returning to

Catania, he traveled — probably again by train — to Syracuse (Siracusa), where the Sicilian tour ends.

Near the very beginning of his travel memoir, Maupassant calls Sicily "a strange and divine museum of architecture," and we are led to believe that the art of building is what led the writer to the island. But near the end he exclaims: "Some people cross continents to go on a pilgrimage to some miraculous statue — as for me, I have brought my devotions to the Venus of Syracuse!" and he adds: "It was she, perhaps, who made up my mind to undertake this voyage; I spoke to her and I dreamt of her at every moment, before having seen her."

Whatever the impetus for extending his Italian tour to Sicily, the writer devoted much space to its ancient and medieval architecture and to two ancient sculptures in local museums. Medieval architecture is discussed first, for that is what he initially encountered in Palermo and its environs, rich in Norman–Byzantine monuments. His discussion of these is prefaced by a lament about contemporary architecture — a "dead" art, no longer capable of conveying beauty, and this comment echoes passages in the first chapter of *La vie errante*, where architecture is called "the most misunderstood and the most forgotten of the arts today," followed by a scathing criticism of the Tour Eiffel. In Sicily, however, thanks to the waves of varying peoples who reached its shores over the centuries, contrasting architectural influences (Greek, Roman, Byzantine, Arab, Norman) have acted on each other to produce monuments of beauty and a unique Sicilian style.

Stepping off the boat in Palermo, Maupassant takes note of its lively streets, the distinctive painted carts, the city's setting and urban plan. But he is in a hurry: "One desire haunted my spirit on this day of arrival. I wanted to see the Palatine Chapel, which I had been told was the marvel of marvels."

And indeed, the writer is not disappointed, calling the chapel "the most surprising religious jewel dreamed up by human thought and executed by the hands of artists." He is startled by the interior sheathing of mosaics, conveyors of religious imagery and yet almost sensual in their luminosity. And he finely observes that the mosaics, combined with the marbles lining the lower walls, form a decorative emphasis, dominant over the architectonic. He later visits the other Norman–Byzantine churches: the Martorana in Palermo and nearby Monreale Cathedral. (He may have also visited Cefalù,[1] on the coast east of Palermo). His comments about Monreale are merely descriptive and pedestrian (but only to a Frenchman could the Pantocrator of the apse have resembled Francis I!). His aesthetic sense, however, is stirred by the cathedral cloister, through its overall proportions and the elegance and delicacy of its colonnettes. And he has praise too for the small cloister of San Giovanni degli Eremiti in Palermo, similarly articulated.

Maupassant's enthusiasm for the architecture and decoration of the Norman–Byzantine school continued a vogue among French writers that had been developing since the 1830s. During the eighteenth and early-nineteenth centuries, these works, with very rare exceptions, had been either ignored or deprecated by writers. But the Romantic movement of the nineteenth century embraced a new sensibility, receptive to medieval art and architecture. Whereas estimates of the Palatine Chapel by travelers, for example, were distinctly negative as late as 1821 and 1822, a new appreciation for that building is found among French writers beginning in the 1830s. Yet even Maupassant's deeply-felt reaction to the cloister of Monreale was anticipated a century earlier by the French painter Jean Houël,who called it "…the most consummate, the most exquisite monument that it is possible to build in this genre."[2]

After the medieval monuments, Maupassant visited the ancient Greek temples of western Sicily. Amid these splendid ruins, the writer could admire a culture long esteemed in France and Europe — he calls the Greeks "the greatest of all artistic peoples." Particularly since the eighteenth century there had been a revived enthusiasm for Greek art, as evidenced in the publications on the monuments of Athens[3] and in the writings of the art historian and archaeologist Johann Joachim Winckelmann. In the publications just mentioned, we find attempted reconstructions of the Greek buildings based on their extant remains, and this archaeological spirit informs some of the writings on the Sicilian monuments in the late eighteenth and nineteenth centuries. But parallel to this were other trends of a more poetic nature, linked to the Romantic movement. There were attempts to find in the Greek ruins a "picturesque" composition, transposable into a painting or engraving, or descriptions of them were used to arouse feelings of melancholy and the theme of *sic transit*. It is interesting that the site which offered the most chaotic heap of ruined stones — Selinunte — was of least interest to Maupassant (the columns of its Temple E were re-erected only in 1958). A writer of the Realistic School, he has little use for the Romantic cult of picturesque ruins and dismisses Selinunte as "[t]his shapeless heap of stones [which] can only be of interest to archaeologists or poetic souls, moved by all traces of the past." What Maupassant particularly finds at the other sites — Segesta and Agrigento, with their standing temples — is a magnificent harmony between the buildings and their settings, and the vivid manner in which these monuments summon up ancient Greece and the antique world itself. And at Segesta, the Greek genius for architectural siting extends to the theater there, placed high on a mountain so that the spectators could look out upon a vast panorama. (Maupassant will find the same approach to theater design at Taormina.)

Back in Palermo, two adventures deserve comment before we track our writer on the other side of the island. A fellow traveler informs him that Richard Wagner completed *Parsifal*, his last opera, while staying in Palermo (1881–82), and Maupassant succeeds in gaining access to Wagner's former hotel suite. The composer had died in 1883, only two years earlier. Maupassant tells us that he was seeking something of that man of genius that must still remain in those rooms, an object which he used or some trace of his occupancy. He opens a mirrored closet and, to his astonishment, "[a] delicious and strong perfume flew out, like the caress of a breeze that had passed over a field of rose-bushes." The hotel manager explained that this was Wagner's linen closet, and that the composer steeped his linen in rose essence, which will never fade away. Maupassant writes:

> I inhaled that breath of flowers, enclosed in that piece of furniture, forgotten there, a captive; and it seemed to me to recover, in truth, something of Wagner, in that exhalation that he loved, a bit of him, a bit of his desire, a bit of his soul, in this trifle of secret and beloved habits that make up the intimate life of a man.

Maupassant had indeed stumbled upon evidence — the significance of which the French writer did not know — related to Wagner's creativity: that in his last years the composer could only work in the presence of certain fragrances. The sense of smell was important to both geniuses, although in different ways, and Maupassant felt he could divine something of Wagner himself in the lingering scent. Interestingly, readers of Maupassant will remember that the description of odors — particularly the aromas of the natural world and women's perfumes — occurs frequently in his fiction, set down in typically lyrical language. (Henry James remarked on Maupassant's sensitivity to scents in his essay on the writer of 1888.[4]) Indeed, in *Sicily* itself we find the following passage (the author is traveling by boat at night through the Straits of Messina to the Aeolian Islands):

> The banks of Sicily and the banks of Calabria give off such a strong scent of flowering orange trees that the entire Straits of Messina are perfumed by them, like a woman's bedroom.

It is tempting to find in the incident concerning Wagner's linen closet the germ of the beautiful passage (although it deals with memory rather than vestiges of the dead) from Maupassant's late novel, *Fort comme la mort* (*Strong as Death*, 1889), in which the protagonist, the aging society painter Olivier Bertin, muses about everyday stimuli which provoke his memories of the past:

> He tried to understand why this bubbling up of his past life had taken place, which already several times, but fewer than today, he had felt and noticed. There was always a reason for these unexpected sequences of thought, a material and simple cause, often an odor, a perfume. How many times had a woman's dress, in passing, sent forth to him, with the evaporated breath of an essence, an entire recollection of obliterated events. At the bottom of old decanters of toiletry, he had also often recovered bits and pieces of his existence; and all the vagrant odors, those of streets, fields,

houses, furniture, the sweet and the bad, the hot odors of summer evenings, the cold odors of winter evenings, always revived in him some distant reminiscences, as if the scents preserved in themselves embalmed dead things, in the fashion of aromatics which preserve mummies.[5]

The other Palermitan adventure — which occupies a number of pages — is a description of the author's descent into the Capuchin catacombs. Of all the monuments that he visited on the island, it is the catacombs that are described in the fullest detail. His morbid fascination with the bizarre displays of the clothed corpses and the placards that indicate their dates of death (some quite recent) surely reveals his awareness of the disease (syphilis) that was gnawing away at his young life and that would cause his tragic death at the age of forty-three. His last creative year was 1890, which saw the publication of *La vie errante* and his last four short stories, two of which are among his greatest: "L'inutile beauté" ("Useless Beauty") and "Le champ d'oliviers" ("The Olive Orchard"), the last declared by the critic Hippolyte Taine to be worthy of Aeschylus.

Although *Sicily* is not divided into sections, its second part may be said to commence with the narrator's description of the Aeolian Islands, located off the northeast coast. (We have previously noted that his train ride from Palermo to Messina — the port of embarkation for the islands — is not mentioned.) The element sulphur — Sicily's most valuable natural resource at the time — forms the connecting motif: from the mines north of Agrigento, with their exploitation of child labor, which he found so shocking, Maupassant transports the reader to those isles, eventually reaching the aptly-named Vulcano, "a fantastic flower of sulphur, blossoming in the ocean midst." He has made this excursion to climb to the crater of the sulphurous volcano, repeating his ascension of Vesuvius when he was in Naples just before arriving in Sicily (not included in *La vie errante*) and anticipating the conquest of Etna, a highlight of the latter part of his travel memoir.

From the open sea, when returning by steamer to Messina, Maupassant first grasps the enormity of Etna and how it dominates the entire island. In Catania he prepares for his ascent. The reader is given information about the effects of the eruptions on the surrounding areas and their long history; a violent one had occurred as recently as 1882. Then Maupassant sets forth. He tells us that "we [the author, Henri Amic, and their guides] made the ascent of this volcano with extreme facility, an ascent somewhat tiring but in no way perilous." This is accurate: even today, tourists are allowed to climb to or near the crater if there are no signs of dangerous volcanic activity (Etna usually emits a continuous stream of smoke). But his account is dramatic and detailed, and difficulties there are aplenty. We are given descriptions of the lava, which supports vegetal growth in its lower reaches; a sudden storm; the icy temperatures; then fields of snow covering the lava, both blinding to the sight. And then, after a night spent in a shelter, the exhausting climb before sunrise on hands and feet through sulphurous exhalations to the crater's edge. In the pre-dawn light, haze followed by clouds gives the impression of standing in the heavens and then at the bottom of a white abyss. Then the sun rises, casting the shadow of Etna over all of Sicily, dissipating the haze and clouds to reveal an immense panorama.

Before this ascent, Maupassant had visited Taormina, his favorite spot in Sicily (as it still is for so many tourists).

As at Segesta, he speaks in the highest terms of the siting of the theater (as did Goethe), which commands a magnificent view, and laments the lack, in the modern world, of the necessary genius to design such an edifice. That is because the Greeks (the theater at Taormina, originally Hellenistic, was actually rebuilt by the Romans) were essentially different beings:

> Those men, those of former times, had soul and eyes that in no way resembled ours, and in their veins, along with their blood, flowed something that has disappeared: love and admiration for the Beautiful.

Syracuse was Maupassant's last destination, his pilgrim's goal, for here in the local museum was the Venus of Syracuse, the headless marble sculpture that he had seen in a photograph, which inflamed his imagination. Indeed, he tells us that he had fallen in love with her.

The pages that Maupassant devotes to this Hellenistic statue — a hymn to sensuality — are of the first importance for our understanding of a major theme of his fictional oeuvre — women's sexuality and psychology. He says that attempts by some writers to poeticize or idealize women actually disfigure them, for to Maupassant the woman is a sensual and sexual being, with a peculiar power to hide and reveal herself simultaneously in her effort to lure the male. He finds these qualities realized to the highest artistic degree in the Venus of Syracuse: the carving and surface quality convey the sensuality of a real, desirable female, and the drapery motif constitutes her snare. The statue also fulfills his Realist credo: "A work of art is only superior if it is, at the same time, a symbol and the exact expression of a reality. The Venus of Syracuse is a woman, and it is also the symbol of the flesh." This statement should be compared to what Maupassant wrote about one of his last short-stories:

"'L'inutile beauté' is the finest story I ever wrote. It is nothing but a symbol" (letter to his publisher Havard, 1889).[6] Readers of that story know, of course, that it is also a searching portrait of a marriage set in late nineteenth-century Paris. In Maupassant's aesthetic, realism of style and symbolic statement are compatible, and their fusion in a work of art is the artist's highest goal.

While contemplating the Venus, Maupassant's mind flashes back to another Hellenistic sculpture, one that he had seen in the museum in Palermo, the Bronze Ram. He remembers it as the most beautiful object in that collection, but also as the disquieting embodiment of "all the animalism of the world." Like the Venus, it encapsulates "the simple beauty of a living creature," and he is left with the burning desire to see these two works of sculpture again.

The Venus of Syracuse and the Bronze Ram were perceived by Maupassant as superb works of visual art symbolizing the elemental forces of creation which, as readers of his great novel *Une Vie* (*A Life*, 1883) will remember, constitute the religion of Baron Le Perthuis des Vauds (Maupassant's alter ego in this instance):

> For his part he belonged with those thinkers of old who worshipped nature, and he was readily affected by the sight of two animals mating. The God to whom he prayed was of a more or less pantheist type, and he was fiercely hostile to the Catholic conception of a God characterized by bourgeois motives, jesuitical wrath, and despotic vengeance, a God who diminished the spectacle of creation as he himself dimly perceived it, that is, of creation as a fateful, limitless, all-powerful force; creation as simultaneously life, light, earth, thought, plant, rock, man, air, beast, star, God, insect; which was created precisely because it was creation, stronger than any individual will, vaster than any

capacity to reason, and productive for no purpose, without cause or temporal limit, in all directions and in all shapes and dimensions, across the infinite reaches of space, as chance and the proximity of world-warming suns dictated.

Creation contained all the seeds of existence, and thought and life developed within it like flowers and fruits upon the trees. For him, therefore, reproduction was the great, general law, a sacred, divine act to be respected, which accomplishes the obscure and constant will of universal being.[7]

Sicily ends with an account of Maupassant's excursion by small open boat along the rivers Cyane (Ciane) and Anapo outside of Syracuse, where grows the papyrus, source of the material which, as he notes, was the preserver of the written word and of human genius — a final act of homage in his Sicilian pilgrimage.

Robert W. Berger

NOTES

In writing this Introduction I am particularly indebted to the magisterial biography by Francis Steegmuller, *Maupassant: A Lion in the Path* (New York: Grosset & Dunlap, 1949).

1. A Norman–Byzantine church with a famous apse mosaic (Pantocrator).

2. *Voyage pittoresque des isles de Sicile, Malthe, et Lipari,* I, 1782.

3. Le Roy, *Les ruines des plus beaux monuments de la Grèce,* 1758; Stuart and Revett, *The Antiquities of Athens,* 1762ff.

4. In *Partial Portraits,* first published in 1888.

5. Translated from the Folio classique edition (Paris: Gallimard, 1983), p. 116.

6. Steegmuller, *Maupassant*, p. 313.

7. *A Life: The Humble Truth*, trans. by Roger Pearson, Oxford World's Classics (Oxford: Oxford University Press, 1999), p. 170.

SICILY

People in France are convinced that Sicily is an uncivilized country, difficult and even dangerous to visit. From time to time, a traveler, who is considered daring, ventures as far as Palermo and returns declaring that it is a very interesting city. And that is all. In what way are Palermo and all of Sicily interesting? We French do not know exactly why. In truth, it is only a question of fashion. That island, pearl of the Mediterranean, is not among the regions that are considered customary to visit, in good taste to know, and like Italy, part of the education of a well-bred man.

From two standpoints, however, Sicily ought to attract travelers: for its natural beauties and its artistic beauties, since they are as singular as they are remarkable. We know how fertile and undulating is that land, which was called the granary of Italy, which all peoples invaded and conquered, one after the other, so violent was their desire to possess it, which made so many men fight and die, as for a beautiful girl ardently desired. It is, like Spain, the land of oranges, its earth in flower, whose air, in springtime, is but perfume; and every evening, above the seas, it kindles the monstrous beacon of Etna, the largest volcano of Europe. But what makes of her, above everything else, an indispensable land to see and one unique in the world, is that she is, from one end to the other, a strange and divine museum of architecture.

Today architecture is dead in this nevertheless still artistic century, which seems to have lost the gift of creating beauty with stone, the mysterious secret of seduction by line, the sense of gracefulness in the monuments. We seem no longer to understand, no longer to know that the mere proportion of a wall can give the spirit the same sensation of artistic joy, the same secret and deep emotion as a masterpiece by Rembrandt, Velázquez or Veronese. Sicily has had the good fortune to be possessed in turn by productive peoples, coming sometimes from the north and sometimes from the south, who have covered its territory with infinitely varied works, where mixed together, in an unexpected and charming way, are the most opposing influences. From that a special art was born, unknown elsewhere, where the Arab influence dominates in the midst of Greek and even Egyptian remembrances; where the severities of Gothic style, brought by the Normans, are tempered by the admirable science of Byzantine ornamentation and decoration.

And it is a delightful happiness to investigate in these exquisite monuments the special imprint of each art, to discern sometimes a detail from Egypt, like the lance-shaped pointed arch brought by the Arabs; vaults in relief or rather in pendentive form, which resemble the stalactites of marine grottoes; sometimes pure Byzantine ornament; or beautiful Gothic friezes which suddenly arouse the memory of tall cathedrals in cold lands, in these slightly low churches, also constructed by Norman princes.

When we have seen all these monuments that — although they belong to different periods and types — have the same character, the same nature, we can say that they are neither Gothic, nor Arab, nor Byzantine, but Sicilian. We can affirm that there exists a Sicilian art and a Sicilian style, always recognizable and assuredly the most charming, the most varied, the most colorful, and the most imaginative of all architectural styles.

It is likewise in Sicily that we find the most magnificent and complete specimens of ancient Greek architecture, in the midst of incomparably beautiful landscapes.

The easiest crossing is from Naples to Palermo. When dis-
embarking from the ship, the movement and the gaiety of
that great city of 250,000 inhabitants,[1] full of shops and
noise is surprising — less agitated than Naples, although
quite as lively. Immediately you stop in front of the first cart
you see. These carts, made of small square boxes perched
high on yellow wheels, are decorated with naïve and bizarre

paintings depicting historical or odd events, adventures of
all sorts, combats, meetings of sovereigns, but especially the
battles of Napoleon I and of the Crusades.[2] A curious piece
of wood and iron supports them on the axle; and the spokes
of their wheels are also finely carved. The beasts who pull
them wear a pompon on their heads and another on the
middle of their backs, and are dressed in stylish and colorful trappings, each piece of leather adorned with a piece of
red wool and small bells. These painted vehicles, curious

3

and original, pass through the streets, attract the eye and the mind, and promenade like rebuses that one is always trying to understand.

The shape of Palermo is very special. The city, set down in the middle of a vast circus of bare mountains — of a gray–blue sometimes nuanced with red — is divided into four quadrants by two large straight streets that cross one another in the center. From this intersection[3] one catches sight of the mountains in three directions, over there, at the end of these immense corridors of houses, and in the fourth direction one sees the sea — a blue patch, harsh blue — which seems very close, as if the city had fallen into it!

One desire haunted my spirit on this day of arrival. I wanted to see the Palatine Chapel, which I had been told was the marvel of marvels.

The Palatine Chapel, the most beautiful in the world, the most surprising religious jewel dreamed up by human thought and executed by the hands of artists, is enclosed within the heavy construction of the Royal Palace, the old fortress built by the Normans.[4]

This chapel has no exterior. You enter it from inside the palace, where you are struck at first by the elegance of the interior courtyard surrounded by columns. A beautiful staircase with straight turns creates a perspective of great unexpected effect. Opposite the entrance door, another door, puncturing the palace wall, opens onto the distant country-side and unlocks suddenly a narrow and deep horizon; it seems to hurl the spirit through this arched opening into countless regions and limitless dreams. This opening seizes the eye and carries it irresistibly towards the blue summit of the mountain glimpsed over there, so far away, so far away, above an immense plain of orange trees.

When you enter the chapel, you at first remain startled, as if in the presence of something surprising whose power you submit to before understanding it. The colorful and calm

beauty, penetrating and irresistible, of that small church, which is the most absolute masterpiece imaginable, leaves you immobile before these walls covered with immense mosaics with gold backgrounds, glistening with a soft clarity, and illuminating the entire monument with a sombre light, immediately transporting thoughts to biblical and divine landscapes where, standing in a sky of fire, all those who were involved in the life of the Man–God are visible.

The impression produced by these Sicilian monuments is so extraordinary because the art of decoration is more impressive at first glance than the art of architecture.

The harmony of lines and proportions is only a frame for the harmony of hues.

Upon entering our Gothic cathedrals, we experience a severe, almost sad, sensation. Their grandeur is imposing, their majesty astonishes, but does not seduce. Here, we are conquered, moved by that something, almost sensual, that color adds to the beauty of forms.

The men who conceived and executed these luminous and sombre churches, however, certainly had an entirely different idea of religious feeling from the architects of the German and French cathedrals; and their special genius was especially uneasy about allowing daylight to enter into these naves so marvelously decorated, so that you do not perceive it, you do not see it: it only steals, glides along the walls, producing mysterious and charming effects. The light seems to come from the walls themselves, from the great golden skies peopled with apostles.

The Palatine Chapel, constructed in 1132 by King Roger II in Norman Gothic style, is a small basilica with a nave and two side-aisles. It is only thirty-three meters long and thirteen meters wide, a plaything therefore, a jewel of a basilica.

Two rows of admirable marble columns, all different in color, lead you beneath the cupola, whence a colossal Christ looks at you, surrounded by angels with wings displayed. The mosaic that forms the background of the left lateral chapel [the north wall of the northern transept arm] is a striking picture. It represents Saint John preaching in the desert. One would say a Puvis de Chavannes, but more colorful, more powerful, more naïve, less studied, made during an age of strong faith by an inspired artist. The apostle is speaking to several people. Behind him, the desert, and all the way back some bluish mountains — those mountains of gentle lines, lost in a haze, which all those who have traveled through the East know well. Above the saint, around the saint, behind the saint, a golden sky, a true miraculous sky where God seems to be present. [5]

Upon returning towards the exit door, you halt beneath the pulpit, a simple square of red marble surrounded by a white marble frieze incrusted with small mosaics and carried by four finely-worked columns. And you marvel over what can be done by taste, the pure taste of an artist, with so little means.

The entire admirable effect of these churches derives, moreover, from the mixture and contrast of marbles and mosaics. That is their characteristic feature. The entire base of the walls, white and decorated only with small designs, with fine embellishments of stone, powerfully brings out, by the very fact of its simplicity, the colorful richness of the large subjects that cover the upper walls.

But you also discover in these small embellishments that run like colored lace along the lower wall — delightful things, as large as the hollow of one's hand: thus two peacocks who, crossing their beaks, carry a cross.

We find in several churches in Palermo this same type of decoration. The mosaics of the Martorana[6] are even, perhaps, more remarkably executed than those in the Palatine Chapel, but you cannot encounter in any other monument the marvellous ensemble that makes this divine masterpiece unique.

🦂

I return slowly to the Hotel des Palmes, which has one of the city's most beautiful gardens, one of those gardens of warm climes, filled with enormous and strange plants. A traveler, seated on a bench, recounts to me in a few moments his year's adventures, then he goes back to stories of past years, and he says, in one sentence: "That was at the time when Wagner lived here."

I was astonished. "Do you mean here, in this hotel?"

"Yes indeed. It was here that he wrote the last notes of *Parsifal* and corrected the proofs."

And I learn that the famous German master had spent an entire winter in Palermo, and that he left this city only a few months before his death. As everywhere, he had displayed here his insufferable character, his extraordinary pride, and left behind the memory of the most unsociable of men.[7]

I wanted to see the apartment that this musician of genius occupied, for it seemed to me that something of him must remain there, and that I would find an object that he liked, a favorite chair, the table where he worked, any sign indicating his passage, the trace of a fancy or the mark of a habit.

I saw nothing at first but a fine hotel apartment. They indicated to me the changes that he had made, they showed me, right in the middle of the room, the location of the large couch where he piled up carpets, bright and adorned with gold.

But I opened the door of the mirrored closet.

A delicious and strong perfume flew out, like the caress of a breeze that had passed over a field of rose bushes.

The hotel manager who escorted me said, "It was in there that he locked away his linen after steeping it in rose essence. That scent will never go away now."

I inhaled that breath of flowers, enclosed in that piece of furniture, forgotten there, a captive; and it seemed to me to recover, in truth, something of Wagner, in that exhalation that he loved, a bit of him, a bit of his desire, a bit of his soul, in this trifle of secret and beloved habits that make up the intimate life of a man.[8]

Then I went out to wander through the city.

No one resembles a Neapolitan less than a Sicilian. In the lower-class Neapolitan one always finds three-fourths of a buffoon. He gestures, is restless, becomes animated without cause, expresses himself as much by gestures as by words, mimes everything he says, always appears amiable through self-interest, gracious by guile as much as by nature, and he responds with pleasant words to disagreeable remarks addressed to him.

But in the Sicilian you already find much of the Arab. He has their grave demeanor even though he has from the Italian a great vivacity of spirit. His native haughtiness, his love of titles, the nature of his pride and even the physiognomy of his face bring him closer also to the Spaniard than to the Italian. But what gives, without ceasing, from the moment one steps on Sicilian soil, the profound impression of the East, is the timbre of the voice, the nasal intonation of the street-criers. You find it everywhere, the sharp note of the

Arab, that note that seems to descend from the forehead into the throat, while in the North it rises from the chest to the mouth. And the drawling song, monotone and sweet, heard while passing the open door of a house, is indeed the same, in its rhythm and accent, as that sung by the horseman dressed in white who guides the travelers across the great bare spaces of the desert.

At the theater, however, the Sicilian becomes again entirely Italian, and it is very interesting for us to attend some operatic performance in Rome, Naples, or Palermo.

All the impressions of the public burst forth immediately as they are felt. Nervous to excess, gifted with an ear as delicate as it is sensitive, loving music to distraction, the entire crowd becomes a sort of vibrating beast that feels but doesn't reason. In five minutes, the same perfomer is applauded with enthusiasm and whistled with frenzy; the crowd stamps with joy or anger, and if some false note escapes from the singer's throat, a strange cry, exasperated, overshrill issues from all mouths at the same time. When the opinions are divided, the shushes and applause mix together. Nothing passes unnoticed in the attentive and quivering house, which shows its feeling at every moment, and which from time to time, seized by a sudden anger, begins to roar like a menagerie of ferocious animals.

Carmen, at this moment, is exciting the Sicilian people, and you hear in the streets from morning to evening the humming of the famous "Toréador" song.

The streets in Palermo are not remarkable in any way. They are wide and beautiful in the wealthy quarters; in the poor sections they resemble all the narrow, torturous and colorful lanes of oriental towns.

The women, wrapped in brightly-colored garments
— red, blue or yellow — chat before their doorways and
observe you passing by with their black eyes, which shine
beneath the forest of their dark hair.

Sometimes, in front of the office of the official lottery, which functions permanently like a religious service and returns large revenues to the government, you witness a funny and typical little scene.

Opposite is the Madonna in her niche, hung on a wall, with the lantern that shines at her feet. A man leaves the office, his lottery ticket in his hand, places a penny in the sacred poor-box, which opens its little black mouth in front of the statue, then he crosses himself with the numbered ticket, which he has just entrusted to the Virgin, while backing it up with alms.

🐾

You can stop here and there before the vendors of Sicilian views, and your eye will fall upon a strange photograph that depicts an underground vault full of the dead — grimacing skeletons, strangely dressed. You read beneath: "Cemetery of the Capuchins."

What can this be? If you ask an inhabitant of Palermo about it, he responds with disgust: "Don't go to see that horror. It's a frightful and barbarous thing, which happily will soon disappear. Moreover, for several years now they no longer do burials there." It is difficult to obtain more detailed and precise information, since most Sicilians seem to express so much horror at these extraordinary catacombs.[9]

Here, however, is what I finally learned. The Capuchin monastery is built on earth that possesses the unusual property of activating the decomposition of dead flesh so strongly that in one year nothing more remains on the bones but a bit of dried and clinging black skin, which sometimes retains the hair of the beard and cheeks. So, they enclose the coffins in small side vaults, each containing eight or ten bodies. At the end of the year, they open the coffins and remove the mummies — frightful mummies, bearded and convulsed, which seem to howl, which seem afflicted by horrible pain. Then they are hung in one of the main galleries, where the families come to visit them from time to time. People who wished to be preserved by this method of drying requested it before they died, and they will remain for eternity, ranged beneath these dark vaults like objects kept in museums, for the consideration of an annual sum paid by their relatives. If the relatives stop paying, the deceased is simply buried in the usual way.

I immediately wanted to visit that grim collection of the deceased.

At the door of a small monastery of modest appearance, an old Capuchin friar in a brown robe received me and preceded me without saying a word, well knowing what the foreigners who came to this place want to see.

We traverse a poor chapel and we slowly go down a broad stone stair. And all of a sudden, I see before us an immense gallery, wide and high, whose walls carry an entire population of skeletons dressed in a bizarre and grotesque manner. Some are hung in the air side by side, others laid out on five stone shelves, placed one above the other from the ground to the ceiling. On the ground stood a compact line of dead bodies, whose frightful heads seem to speak. Some are wasted by hideous vegetation, which deforms even more the jaws and the bones; others have kept their hair, others a bit of moustache, others a wisp of beard.

These over here gaze up into the air with their empty eyes, those over there look down; here are some who seem to laugh outrageously, there are others who are contorted by pain; all seem driven mad by a superhuman terror.

And they are clothed — these dead bodies, these poor hideous and ridiculous dead bodies — dressed by their

families, who took them from their coffins so they could take their places in this dreadful assembly. Almost all of them wear black gowns with hoods, sometimes drawn over their heads. But there are some they wished to dress more sumptuously, and the miserable skeleton, covered with a Greek embroidered cap and wrapped in the dressing-gown of a rich *rentier*, stretched out on his back, seems to sleep a terrifying and comical sleep.

Blind-men's placards, hanging from their necks, bear their names and dates of death. These dates send shivers through the bones. You read: 1880, 1881, 1882.

Here then is a man, he who was a man eight years ago? He lived, laughed, spoke, ate, drank, was full of joy and hope. And there he is! In front of this double line of beings without number, coffins and boxes are piled up, luxury coffins of black wood, with copper ornaments and little glass panes for looking inside. You would think that they are trunks, valises of savages, bought in some bazaar by those embarking on the long voyage, as people used to say.

14

But other galleries open to the right and left, indefinitely prolonging this immense subterranean cemetery. Here are the women, yet more ludicrous than the men, for they have been decked out coquettishly. Their heads face toward you, clasped in lace- and ribbon-trimmed bonnets, a snow-like whiteness around these black, rotten faces, wasted by the strange workings of the earth. The hands, similar to the cut roots of trees, emerge from the sleeves of new robes, and the stockings that cover the bones of the legs seem empty. Sometimes the dead body only wears shoes — big, big shoes for these poor dry feet.

Here are girls, hideous girls, in their white finery, bearing metal crowns on their heads, symbols of innocence. You would call them old, very old, to such a degree do they grimace. They were sixteen, eighteen, twenty years old. How horrible!

But we come to a gallery full of small glass coffins — these are the children. The bones, barely firm, could not endure. And it is hard to really know what you see, to such an extent are they deformed, crushed and frightful, the pitiable little things. But tears come to your eyes, for the mothers have dressed them in the little costumes that they wore during the last days of their lives. And they come to see them thus again, their children!

Often by the side of the cadaver, a photograph is hung that shows him as he was, and nothing is more piercing, more terrifying than this contrast, than this juxtaposition, than the ideas aroused in us by this comparison.

We traverse a gallery that is darker, lower, and seems reserved for the poor. In a dark corner are about twenty together, hung beneath a dormer window, which throws the outside air upon them in great sudden gusts. They are dressed in a sort of black cloth tied at the feet and neck, one leaning on the other. They look as if they are shivering, that they want to escape, that they are crying out: "Help!" They seem to be the drowned crew of some ship, still battered by the wind, wrapped in the dark and tarred canvas that sailors wear during storms, and still shaken by the terror of the last moment when the waters seized them.

Here is the priests' quarter. A great gallery of honor! At first sight, they seem more terrible to look at than the others, covered thus with their sacred ornaments — black, red and violet. But while considering them one after the other, a nervous and irresistible laughter seizes you in front of their bizarre and sinisterly comic poses. Here are some who chant; there are some who pray. Their heads have been raised and their hands crossed. Their fleshless heads are covered with the biretta of the officiating priest and placed there it sometimes slopes over the ear in a droll manner, sometimes it slips down on the nose. It is the carnival of death rendered more ludicrous by the gilt richness of the priestly garments.

From time to time, it seems that a head rolls to the ground, the neck cords having been gnawed by mice. Thousands of mice live in this human charnel-house.

They show me a man who died in 1882. A few months before, jolly and in good health, he came to select his place, accompanied by a friend: "I shall be over there," he said and he laughed.

The friend comes back alone now and, for hours at a time, looks at the motionless skeleton standing in the selected spot.

On certain holidays, the catacombs of the Capuchins are open to the crowd. A drunken man once fell asleep in that place and awoke in the middle of the night. He called, he yelled, lost in fright, running in all directions trying to escape. But no one heard him. He was found in the morning, clinging so tightly to the bars of the entrance grille, that it took long efforts to detach him from it.

He was insane.

Since that day they have hung a large bell near the doorway.

🐾

After this grim visit, I felt a desire to see flowers, and I was driven to Villa Tasca, whose gardens, placed in the middle of a grove of orange-trees, are full of admirable tropical plants.[10]

While returning to Palermo, I viewed to my left a small town towards the middle of a mountain, and, on the summit, a ruin. That town is Monreale and that ruin, Castellaccio, the last refuge, I am told, where the Sicilian bandits hid.[11]

The master poet Théodore de Banville has written a treatise on French prosody that should be known by heart by all those who have the intention of making two words rhyme together. One of the chapters of this excellent book is entitled "On Poetic License"; we turn the page and read: "There is none."

Thus, when one arrives in Sicily, one asks, sometimes with curiosity, sometimes with inquietude: "Where are the brigands?" and everyone replies to you: "There aren't any more."

There aren't any more, in fact, for the last five or six years. Thanks to the concealed complicity of several great landowners, whose interests they often served and whom they also often fleeced, they were able to hold out in the Sicilian mountains until the arrival of General Pallavicini, who still is in command in Palermo.[12] But that officer pursued them and dealt with them so vigorously that the last disappeared in a short time.

It is true that there are often armed assaults and killings in this country; but these are ordinary crimes, committed by isolated malefactors and not by organized bands as formerly.

In short, Sicily is as safe for the traveler as England, France, Germany or Italy, and those who desire adventures of the Fra Diavolo[13] sort will have to go search for them elsewhere.

In truth, one is safe almost everywhere, except in the big cities. If one counted the travelers stopped and plundered by bandits in wild countries, those killed by wandering desert tribes, and if one compared the accidents that occurred in the lands reputed dangerous with those that take place in one month in London, Paris or New York, one would see how without danger the dreaded regions are.

Moral: If you are seeking thrusts of the knife and hold-ups, go to Paris or London, but don't come to Sicily. One can in this country travel by road day and night without escort and unarmed; one only encounters people full of goodwill for the stranger, with the exception of certain postal and telegraph employees. I say this only for those of Catania, however.

One the mountains that dominates Palermo supports half-way up a small town famous for its old monuments, Monreale; and it was on the outskirts of that high-perched town that the last malefactors of the island used to operate. They have kept the custom of placing sentinels all along the route that leads there. Do they want to reassure or frighten the travelers by that? I don't know.

The soldiers, spaced at all the turnings of the road, remind you of the legendary sentinel of the minister of war in France. Every day for ten years, without anyone knowing why, they placed a sentry in the corridor leading to the minister's apartment. His mission was to keep all the passers-by away from the wall. Then a new minister, of an inquisitive turn of mind and successor to fifty others who had passed in front of the sentry without astonishment, asked the reason for that surveillance. No one could tell him why, neither the head of the cabinet nor the bureau-chiefs pasted to their armchairs for a half-century. But an usher, a man of good memory who perhaps wrote his memoirs, recalled that a soldier had been placed there in former times because they had just repainted the wall, and that the minister's wife, not forewarned, had stained her dress. The paint had dried but the sentinel still remained.

Thus the brigands have disappeared, but the sentinels remain along the road to Monreale. It turns all along the mountain, that road, and finally arrives in the town, which is very quaint, highly colored and very dirty. The streets in the form of stairs seem paved with pointed teeth. The men's heads are wrapped in red handkerchiefs in the Spanish style.

Here is the cathedral,[14] a great monument more than a hundred meters long in the form of a Latin cross, with three apses and a nave with side aisles separated by eighteen columns of oriental granite resting on a white marble base and a square plinth of gray marble. The entrance portal, truly admirable, frames magnificent bronze doors made by *Bonannus, Civus Pisanus.*

The interior of this monument displays the most complete, the richest and the most impressive mosaic decoration on a gold ground.

These mosaics,[15] the most extensive in Sicily, entirely cover the walls over a surface of 6,400 meters.[16] Just imagine these immense and superb decorations presenting, throughout the entire church, the legendary stories of the Old Testament, the Messiah, and the apostles. Against the golden sky, which opens up a fantastic horizon, all around the nave and side aisles, you see standing out clearly, larger than life, the prophets announcing God, the Christ who has come, and those who lived in His time. In the depth of the apse, an immense figure of Jesus, resembling Francis I, dominates the entire church — seems to fill it and overwhelm it, so enormous and powerful is that strange image.

It is regrettable that the ceiling, destroyed by a fire, should have been remade in the crudest manner. The loud tone of the gilding and the too-vivid colors are most disagreeable to the eye.

Very near the cathedral one enters the old Benedictine cloister.[17]

Let those who love cloisters go for a stroll in that one, and they will forget almost all the others previously seen.

How can you not adore cloisters, those tranquil places — enclosed and cool — devised, it would seem, to produce the thoughts, deep and clear, that flow from lips while you walk at a slow pace under the long, melancholy arcades?

How they appear well-fashioned to give rise to daydreaming, these stone walks, these walks with slender columns enclosing a little garden that rests the eye without bewildering it, without hurrying it, without distracting it!

But the cloisters of our country sometimes have a severity — a bit too monkish, a bit too sad — even the pretttiest like the one at Saint-Wandrille in Normandy. They rend the heart and darken the soul.

Go visit the desolate cloister of the Carthusian monastery of La Verne in the wild mountains of the Maures. It chills the marrow of one's bones.

The marvellous cloister of Monreale, on the other hand, transmits to the soul such a feeling of gracefulness that one would like to remain there almost indefinitely. It is very large, perfectly square, of a delicate and fine elegance; and

he who hasn't seen it cannot understand what the harmony of a colonnade is. The exquisite proportions, the incredible slenderness of all these slight columns, standing two by two, side by side, all different, some clad in mosaics, others plain; the latter covered with sculptures of incomparable fineness, the former adorned with a simple design in stone that climbs around them, twisting round like a creeping plant, astonishing one's sight, then charming it, enchanting it, producing that artistic joy that things of absolute taste engender in the soul through the eyes.

And like all these delicate paired colonnettes, all the capitals, of charming workmanship, are different. You marvel at the same time — a very rare thing — at the admirable effect of the whole and at the perfection of the detail.

You cannot look at this true masterpiece of graceful beauty without recalling the verses of Victor Hugo on the Greek artist who could put:

Something beautiful like a human smile
On the profile of the Propylaea.[18]

This divine covered walk is enclosed within high walls, very old, with pointed arcades; that is all that remains today of the monastery.

Sicily is the homeland, the true, the only homeland of colonnades. All the inner courtyards of the old palaces and old houses of Palermo enclose some admirable ones, which would be famous elsewhere than in this island so rich in monuments.

The small cloister of the church of San Giovanni degli Eremiti[19] — one of the oldest Norman churches of eastern character, although less remarkable than Monreale — is yet quite superior to all that I know as comparable.

On leaving the monastery, you enter the garden, which commands a view of the entire valley full of orange trees in bloom. A continual breeze rises from the scented forest, a breeze that intoxicates the spirit and troubles the senses. The desire, vague and poetic, that forever haunts the human soul, that prowls about, maddening and unattainable, seems about to be attained. That scent suddenly enveloping you, mixing the delicate sensation of perfumes with the artistic joy of the spirit, casts you for a few seconds into a comfort of mind and body that is almost happiness.

I raise my eyes towards the high mountain dominating the city and I perceive on the summit the ruin I had seen the day before. A friend accompanying me questions the local residents and they tell us that this old castle was indeed the last refuge of the Sicilian brigands. Even today, almost no one climbs up to that ancient fortress, named Castellaccio.[20] Even the path is scarcely known, for it is on a peak difficult to access. But we want to go there. A resident of Palermo, who greets us warmly, insists on providing us with a guide, but not being able to find one who seems to him to know the way, he speaks, without informing us, to the chief of police. And soon an official, whose profession we don't know, begins to ascend the mountain with us.

But he himself hesitates and takes on another companion along the way, a new guide who will lead the first one. Then both ask for directions from peasants they meet, from women who pass by, driving an ass before them. Finally, a parish priest advises us to go straight ahead. And we climb, followed by our guides. The road becomes almost impassable. We have to scale rocks, lifting ourselves by the strength of our wrists. And that lasts a long time. A burning sun, a sun of the Orient, falls perpendicularly upon our heads.

Finally we reach the top, in the midst of a surprising and superb chaos of enormous stones that emerge from the ground, gray, bare, round or pointed, and which imprison the wild and tumbledown castle in a strange host of rocks extending far away on all sides around the walls.

The view from this summit is one of the most thrilling that you can discover. All around the rough mountain, deep valleys are hollowed out, enclosed by other mountains, opening an infinite horizon of peaks and summits towards the interior of Sicily. Facing us is the sea; at our feet, Palermo. The city is surrounded by that forest of orange trees that they call the Golden Shell — La Conca d'Oro — and that forest of black verdure spreads out, like a dark stain, to the feet of the grayish mountains, the reddish-brown mountains, which seem burnt, consumed and gilded by the sun, so bare and colored are they.

One of our guides has disappeared. The other follows us among the ruins. They are beautifully wild and extremely vast. While exploring them you feel as if no one visits here. Everywhere the hollow ground sounds beneath your steps; in spots you see the entrance to underground places. The man examines them with interest and tells us that plenty of brigands lived down there some years earlier. That was their best refuge and the most feared. Just as we are about to descend, the first guide reappears, but we refuse his services and discover without any difficulty a very accessible path that even women could follow.

❦

The Sicilians seem to have taken pleasure in exaggerating and multiplying the stories about bandits in order to frighten foreigners; and even today people hesitate to visit that island, which is as tranquil as Switzerland.

Here is one of the latest adventures credited to these malevolent prowlers. I guarantee its truthfulness.

A very distinguished entomologist of Palermo, Signor Ragusa, had discovered a beetle that was mistaken for a long time for the *Polyphylla Olivieri*. Then a German scientist, Herr Kraatz, recognizing that it belonged to an entirely different species, wanted to acquire some specimens and wrote to one of his friends in Sicily, Signor di Stephani, who addressed himself in turn to Signor Giuseppe Miraglia, to ask him to capture a few of these insects for him. But they had disappeared from the coast. Exactly at that moment, Signor Lombardo Martorana of Trapani announced to Signor di Stephani that he had just caught more than fifty *Polyphylla*.

Signor di Stephani hastened to inform Signor Miraglia by the following letter:

My Dear Giuseppe,

The *Polyphylla Olivieri*, having learned of your murderous intentions, has taken another route and has gone to take refuge on the coast of Trapani, where my friend Lombardo has already captured more than fifty of these individuals.

Here the story takes on the tragicomic features of an improbable epic.

At that time, the outskirts of Trapani were overrun, it seems, by a bandit named Lombardo.

Now Signor Miraglia threw his friend's letter in the wastebasket. The servant emptied the basket in the street, then the garbage-collector passed by and carried what he had gathered to the open country. A peasant, seeing in the fields a fine blue paper, which was scarcely rumpled, picked it up and put it in his pocket either out of precaution or an instinctive desire for gain.

25

Several months had passed, when that man was called to the tax-office and accidentally let that letter fall to the floor. A policeman seized it and presented it to the judge, who stopped short over the words: "murderous intentions," "taken another route," "refuge," "captured," "Lombardo." The peasant was put in jail, questioned, put in solitary confinement. He admitted nothing. They guarded him and a strict investigation was opened. The magistrates published the suspect letter but, since they had read "Petronilla Olivieri" instead of "Polyphylla," the entomologists were not troubled.

At last they finally deciphered the signature of Signor di Stephani, who was called to the court. His explanations were not accepted. Signor Miraglia, summoned in turn, finally cleared up the mystery.

By that time, the peasant had been in jail for three months.

One of the last Sicilian brigands was therefore, in truth, a species of maybug known by men of science under the name of *Polyphylla Ragusa.*

Nothing is less dangerous today than to travel through this dreaded Sicily, whether by train, by horse, or even on foot. All of the most interesting excursions, moreover, can be made almost entirely by rail. The first one to make is to the temple of Segesta.[21]

So many poets have sung of Greece, that each one of us carries an image of it in our minds; each of us believes we know it a little; each of us perceives it in dreaming as we desire it to be. For me, Sicily realized this dream; it has shown me Greece; and when I think of that so-artistic land, it seems to me that I perceive some great mountains with soft lines, with classic lines, and, on the summits, temples, those severe temples, slightly heavy perhaps, but admirably majestic, which you meet with everywhere on this island.

Everyone has seen Paestum and admired the three superb ruins cast upon that bare plain, which the sea extends into the distance and which is enclosed on the other side by a wide circle of bluish mountains. But if the Temple of Neptune is more perfectly preserved and purer — so they say — than the Sicilian temples, the latter are sited in landscapes so marvellous, so unexpected, that nothing in the world can make us imagine the impression that they actually leave on the mind.

When you leave Palermo, you first come upon the vast forest of orange trees called the Golden Shell. Then the railroad follows the shore, a shore-line of reddish mountains and red crags. The line finally bends towards the interior of the island and you get out at the Alcamo–Calatafimi station.

Then you go on through a countryside broadly heaved up, like a sea of monstrous and immobile waves. No woods, few trees, but vineyards and crops; and the road climbs between two uninterrupted rows of flowering aloe. You might think that a password had been exchanged among them so that they pushed towards the sky, in the same year, almost on the same day, the enormous and bizarre column that the poets have sung about so much. You follow as far as the eye can see the infinite troop of these war-like plants, thick, pointed, armed and cuirassed — they seem to carry battle banners.

After about two hours on the road, you suddenly perceive two high mountains, linked by a gentle slope, rounded in crescent-shape from one summit to the other, and, in the middle of this crescent, the profile of a Greek temple — one of those powerful and beautiful monuments that the divine people erected to its human gods.

You must go around one of these mountains by a long detour, and you again discover the temple, which now presents itself frontally. It seems to lean against the mountain, although a deep ravine separates the two; but the mountain spreads out behind and above it, enclosing it, surrounding it, seeming to shelter it, to caress it. And it stands out admirably, with its thirty-six Doric columns, upon the immense green drapery, which serves as a backdrop for the enormous monument, standing all alone in that limitless countryside.

When you see this grandiose and simple landscape, you feel that only a Greek temple could be placed there, and only on that spot. The master designers who have taught that art to humanity demonstrate, especially in Sicily, what a profound and refined knowledge they possessed of the effect of the setting. I will soon speak about the temples of

Agrigento. Segesta seems to have been placed at the foot of that mountain by a man of genius who had a revelation about the exact point where it had to be erected. It animates all by itself the immensity of the landscape; it makes it living and divinely beautiful.

Upon the summit of the mountain, whose base one follows to reach the temple, one finds the ruins of the theater.[22]

When you visit a land that the Greeks have inhabited or colonized, look for their theaters to find the most beautiful viewing points. If they sited their temples exactly on the spot where they could give the greatest effect, where they could best adorn the horizon, they sited their theaters, to the contrary, exactly on the spot where the eye could be stirred the most by the views. The theater of Segesta, on the summit of a mountain, forms the center of an amphitheater of mountains whose circumference reaches at least 150 to 200

kilometers. You discover still other peaks far off, behind the
first ones. And across a wide bay facing you, the sea appears,
blue among the green crests.

🦎

The day following the visit to Segesta, one can visit Selinunte,[23] an immense heap of collapsed columns, fallen
sometimes in a row, side-by-side, like dead soldiers, sometimes overthrown into chaos.

These ruins of giant temples, the most vast in Europe,
fill up an entire plain and also cover a small hill at the end
of the plain. They follow the shore, a long beach of pale
sand where a few fishing boats are stranded, without any
indication of where the fishermen live. This shapeless heap
of stones, however, can only be of interest to archaeologists
or poetic souls, moved by all traces of the past.

🦎

But Agrigento, the ancient Agrigentum, sited, like Selinunte, on the southern coast of Sicily, offers the most astonishing ensemble of temples that you can experience.[24]

On the ridge of a long hill — stony, all barren and red (of a fiery red); without a blade of grass, without a bush; and dominating the sea, the beach and the port — three superb temples, seen from below, display their great silhouettes of stone against the blue sky of southern climes.

They appear standing in the air in the midst of a magnificent and desolate landscape. All is dead, arid and yellow around them, in front of them and behind them. The sun has burned, eaten the earth. Is it indeed the sun that has thus consumed the ground or the fire down deep, which forever burns in the veins of this island of volcanoes? For everywhere around Agrigento stretches the strange land of sulphur mines. Here, everything is sulphurous, the earth, the stones, the sand, everything.

The temples themselves, eternal homes of the gods — dead like their brothers, the ancient Greeks — remain

31

on their wild hill, distant one from another by about a half kilometer. Here is first the one of Juno Lacinia, which contained, it was said, the famous painting of Juno by Zeuxis, who had selected as models the five most beautiful girls of Agrigento.[25]

Then the temple of Concord, one of the best preserved of antiquity because it served as a church during the Middle Ages.[26] Further on the remains of the temple of Hercules.[27]

And finally the gigantic temple of Jupiter [Olympian Zeus], praised by Polybius and described by Diodorus, built in the fifth century, and containing thirty-eight half-columns, each six and a half meters in circumference.[28] A man can stand up in each vertical groove.

Seated on the side of the road that runs to the foot of that surprising hill, you pause to dream before these admirable mementos of the greatest of all artistic peoples. It seems that all Olympus is before us, the Olympus of Homer, of Ovid, of Virgil, the Olympus of gods delightful, sensual, passionate like us, fashioned like us, who poetically personify all the tenderness of our hearts, all the dreams of our souls and all the instincts of our senses.

It is all of antiquity that rises before this ancient sky. A powerful and strange emotion penetrates you, as well as a desire to kneel before these august remains, before these remnants left by the masters of our masters.

This Sicily is indeed, above all, a divine land, because if you find there those last abodes of Juno, Jupiter, Mercury or Hercules, you also encounter the most remarkable Christian churches in the world. And the memory that remains with you of the cathedrals of Cefalù or of Monreale, as well as of the Palatine Chapel — that unique wonder — is even more powerful and more vivid than the memory of the Greek monuments.

At the end of the hill of Agrigento's temples an astonishing region commences. It seems like Satan's true realm, for if — as was formerly believed — the devil inhabits a vast underground country, full of melting sulphur, where he boils the damned, Sicily is surely the place where he has established his mysterious abode.

Sicily supplies almost all of the world's sulphur. You find sulphur mines by the thousands on that island of fire.

But first, several kilometers from the town, you come upon a strange hill called Maccaluba, made of clay and limestone and covered with small cones two to three feet high. You would think they were blisters — a monstrous sickness of nature — for from all the cones flows hot mud, like a frightful suppuration of the soil. And sometimes they hurl stones to a great height, and they roar in a strange way while blowing gases. They seem to growl — filthy, shameful little volcanos, spurious, leprous burst abcesses.

Next we go to visit the sulphur mines. We enter the mountains. Before us lies a region of real desolation, a wretched land, which seems cursed, condemned by nature. The small valleys open, gray, yellow, stony, sinister, bearing the mark of divine reprobation, with a proud quality of solitude and poverty.

Finally you perceive, from place to place, some sordid, very low buildings. These are the mines. They reckon, it seems, more than a thousand of them in this end of the district.

Upon entering within the perimeter of one of them, you first notice a singular hilllock, grayish and smoking. It is a true source of sulphur, the result of human labor.

Here is how it is obtained. The sulphur, drawn from the mines, is blackish, mixed with earth, limestone, etc., and forms a sort of hard and brittle stone. As soon as it is brought out of the mines, it is formed into a high mound, then a fire is set in the middle of it. This fire — slow, continuous, deep — consumes, for weeks at a time, the center of the artificial mountain and releases the pure sulphur, which melts and then flows, like water, through a small drain.

The resulting product is processed again in vats, where it is boiled and finally clarified.

The mine where the extraction took place resembles all mines. You descend by a narrow stair, with enormous and unequal steps, into wells hollowed out in the midst of the sulphur. The superposed floors communicate by wide holes which supply air to the deepest. You choke, however, at the bottom of the descent; you choke and you suffocate, asphyxiated by the sulphurous emanations and by the ter-rible stove-like heat, which causes the heart to beat and covers the skin with sweat.

From time to time you encoun-ter, climbing up the rough staircase, a troop of children loaded with baskets. They pant and gasp, these wretched ur-chins, weighed down under their loads. They are ten, twelve years old, and they repeat, fifteen times in a single day, the abominable voyage, in return for one sou each trip down. They are small, thin, yellow, with huge, shining eyes, with delicate faces with thin lips, showing their teeth, brilliant like their glances.

This revolting exploitation of children is one of the most painful things that one can see.[29]

But there exists on another coast of the island, or rather some hours from the coast, a natural phenomenon so prodigious that one forgets, when one has seen it, these poisoned mines where children are killed. I wish to talk about the island of Vulcano,[30] a fantastic flower of sulphur, blossoming in the ocean midst. You depart from Messina, at midnight, in a filthy steamboat, where the first-class passengers don't even find benches on the deck where they can sit. No puff of a breeze; only the movement of the vessel stirs the calm air asleep on the water.

The banks of Sicily and the banks of Calabria give off such a strong scent of flowering orange trees, that the entire Straits of Messina are perfumed by them, like a woman's bedroom. Soon the city grows distant, we pass between Scylla and Charybdis, the mountains sink behind us, and above them appears the flattened and snowy summit of Etna, which seems bedecked with silver under the light of the full moon.

Afterwards you sleep a bit, lulled by the monotone sound of the propeller, only to reopen your eyes to the light of the dawning day.

Here, over there, facing us, the Lipari or Aeolian Islands. The first on the left and the last on the right throw a thick white smoke upon the sky. They are Vulcano and Stromboli. Between these two volcanos you can pick out Lipari, Filicudi, Alicudi and some very low, small islands.

And the vessel will soon be in front of the small island and the small town of Lipari.

A few white houses at the foot of a large green coast. Nothing more, no inn, for no foreigner arrives on this island.

It is fertile, charming, surrounded by admirable rocks, of bizarre shape, of a strong yet soft red. You find there thermal waters, which were formerly frequented, but Bishop Todaso had the baths, which had been constructed, destroyed in order to remove the influence of foreigners from his native land.

Lipari is capped, at the north, by a strange white mountain, which you would take from afar to be a mountain of snow, were it under a colder sky. Pumice-stone is supplied to the whole world from there.

But I rent a boat to go and visit Vulcano.

Swept along by four oarsmen, the boat follows the fertile coast planted with vines. The reflections of the red rocks are strange upon the blue sea. Here is the little strait that

separates the two islands. The cone of Vulcano rises from the waves, like a volcano submerged up to its head.

It is a small, wild island, whose summit reaches to about 400 meters and whose surface is about 20 square kilometers. Before reaching it, you go around another small island, Vulcanello, which suddenly arose from the sea circa 200 BC,[31] and which is united to its elder brother by a narrow tongue of land, swept by the waves on stormy days.

Here we are at the farther end of a flat bay, facing a smoking crater. At its foot, a house inhabited by an Englishman who, it appears, is sleeping at this moment. Without this circumstance I would not have been able to climb the volcano, which this manufacturer exploits. But he is sleeping and I cross a large kitchen garden, then some vineyards, property of the Englishman, then a real forest of Spanish gorse in bloom. You might think it was an immense yellow scarf, coiled around the pointed cone, whose top is also yellow, of a blinding yellow under the dazzling sun. And I begin to climb by a narrow path that winds through the ashes and the lava — twisting and turning, steep, slippery and difficult. Sometimes, as in Switzerland you see torrents falling from summits, you perceive an immobile cascade of sulphur that pours out through a crevice.

You might think they were streams of fairy-land, of congealed light, or fluid rays of the sun.

Finally on the crest I reach a large platform surrounding the large crater. The ground trembles, and before me an immense jet of flame and steam escapes violently through a hole as large as a man's head, while I can see spread out, from the rim of that hole, the liquid sulphur, gilded by the fire. It forms around this fantastic spring a yellow lake, which hardens very rapidly.

Further away, other crevices also spit forth white vapors that slowly rise into the blue sky.

SICILY

I advance fearfully over the hot cinders and lava up to the edge of the large crater. Nothing more astonishing can strike the human eye.

At the bottom of that immense pit called "la Fossa" —500 meters wide and about 200 meters deep — about ten giant fissures and some vast round holes vomit forth fire, smoke and sulphur with a terrific noise like the boilers of steam engines. You go down along the walls of that abyss and walk on up to the edge of the furious mouths of the volcano. Everything is yellow around me, under my feet and over me, a blinding yellow, a maddening yellow. Everything is yellow: the ground, the high walls, and the sky itself. The yellow sun casts into that roaring gulf its intense light, which the heat of that pit of sulphur renders painful like a burn. And you see the yellow liquid boiling, flowing; you see strange crystals flowering, dazzling and strange acids frothing at the edge of the red rims of the furnace.

The Englishman, who is sleeping at the foot of the mountain, gathers, processes and sells these acids, these liquids, everything that the crater vomits forth. It seems all of it is worth money, a lot of money. I return slowly, winded, panting, suffocated by the unendurable fumes of the volcano; and soon, upon climbing back to the summit of the cone, I see all the Aeolian islands scattered about on the waves.

Over there, in front, rises Stromboli, while behind me, gigantic Etna seems to gaze at her children and grand-children, far away.

From the boat, on my return trip, I discovered an island hidden behind Lipari. The boatman called it Salina. It is there that they gather the grapes for Malmsey wine.

I wanted to drink a bottle of that famous wine at its very source. It is like syrup of sulphur. It is indeed the wine of volcanos: thick, sugary, golden and so sulphurous that the taste remains on your palate until evening — the devil's wine.

🐜

The filthy steamer that brought me takes me back. First I gaze at Stromboli, a round and high mountain with smoking

summit, its base submerged in the sea. It is nothing but an enormous cone that rises from the water. On its sides you espy a few houses hung like sea shells on the ridge of a rock. Then my eyes turn towards Sicily, my return destination, and they see only Etna crouched upon her, crushing her with its formidable, monstrous weight and dominating with its snow-covered summit all the other mountains of the island.

They look like dwarfs, those great mountains, below it; and Etna itself seems low, being so wide and weighty. In order to grasp the dimensions of this heavy giant, you have to see it from the open sea.

On the left, the hilly shores of Calabria reveal themselves, and the Straits of Messina open like the mouth of a river. We soon go through them to enter the port. There is nothing of interest in Messina. On the same day we take the train to Catania. It follows a wonderful coastline, going round strange gulfs peopled by small white villages at the rear of the bays, at the edge of the sands. Here is Taormina.

🦎

Were a man to spend only one day in Sicily and ask, "What must one see?" I would answer him without hesitation, "Taormina."

It is only a landscape, but a landscape where you find everything on earth that seems made to seduce the eyes, the mind and the imagination.

The village is suspended upon a large mountain, as if it had rolled down from the summit. Although it contains some pretty remains from the past, we merely pass through it and go to the Greek theater to see the sunset.

I have said, in speaking of the theater of Segesta, that the Greeks — those incomparable scenic designers — knew how to select the unique site where the theater should be built, that site made for satisfying the artistic senses.

The one in Taormina is so marvellously placed that there cannot be another comparable site in the whole world.[32] After you enter the precinct and visit the stage — the only one that has survived in good condition — you climb the benches — sunken and grass-covered, formerly occupied by the public, capable of holding 35,000 spectators — and you look around.

At first you see the ruin — melancholy, stately, crumbling — where some pleasing columns of white marble remain standing, still quite white, topped with their capitals;

then, above the walls, you perceive, down below, the sea, stretching as far as the eye can see: the shore, which extends to the horizon, strewn with enormous rocks, bordered with gilded sand and peopled with white villages; then, over there, on the right, above everything, dominating all, filling half the sky with its mass — Etna, covered with snow and exhaling smoke.[33]

Where are the nations of today which would know how to create such things? Where are the men who would know how to construct, for the entertainment of crowds, edifices like this one?

Those men, those of former times, had soul and eyes that in no way resembled ours, and in their veins, along with their blood, flowed something that has disappeared: love and admiration for the Beautiful.

But we are leaving for Catania; from there I plan to climb the volcano.

From time to time, you perceive it between two mountains, topped by a motionless cloud of vapors escaping from the crater. Everywhere around us, the soil is brown, the color of bronze. The train runs along a bank of lava.

The monster is far away, however, perhaps thirty-six or forty kilometers distant. Then you understand how enormous it is. From its black and enormous mouth it has vomited forth, from time to time, a burning wave of bitumin which, flowing down its gentle or rapid slopes, filled valleys, buried villages, drowned men like a river. It ended by extinguishing itself in the sea, all the while driving it back before

it. These waves — slow, muddy and red — have formed cliffs, mountains, ravines; becoming dark upon hardening, they have thrown down all around the immense volcano a black and strange land, full of crevices, dented, tortuous, improbable, designed by the vagaries of eruptions and the appalling fantasy of hot lavas.

Sometimes Etna remains quiet for centuries, merely blowing into the sky the heavy fumes of its crater. Then, under the rain and under the sun, the lava of old flows becomes pulverized, forming a sort of cinder, a sandy and black earth, from which grow olive, orange and lemon trees, pomegranate trees, vines, crops.

Nothing is so green, so pretty, so charming as Acireale, set in the midst of a forest of orange and olive trees. Then, sometimes, through the trees, you see again a wide black flow, which has withstood time, which has kept the shapes of all the bubblings up — extraordinary outlines, appearances of interlaced beasts, twisted limbs.

🐎

Here is Catania, a vast and beautiful city, constructed entirely on lava. From the windows of the Grand Hotel we discern the whole summit of Etna.

Before ascending it, let us write its history in a few lines.

The ancients called it Vulcan's workshop. Pindar described the eruption of 476,[34] but Homer does not mention Etna as a volcano. It had, however, already before historical time, forced the Sicans[35] to flee far from it. About eighty eruptions are known.

The most violent were those of 396, 126 and 122 BC, then those of 1169, 1329, 1537 and especially that of 1669, which chased more than 27,000 people from their homes and caused a great number to perish.

It was then that two high mountains, the Monti Rossi, rose suddenly from the earth.

In 1693 an eruption, accompanied by a terrible earthquake, destroyed about forty towns and buried close to 100,000 people under the debris. In 1755, another eruption again caused frightful havoc. Those of 1792, 1843, 1852, 1865, 1874, 1879 and 1882 were equally violent and murderous. Sometimes the lava shoots up from the large crater; sometimes it opens up outlets fifty to sixty meters wide on the sides of the mountain and escapes from these crevices, flowing towards the plain. On May 26, 1879, the lava — first emerging from the crater of 1874 — soon gushed forth from a new cone, 170 meters high, rising by its force to an altitude of about 2,450 meters. It descended rapidly, crossing the road from Linguaglossa to Rondazzo, halting near the Alcantara River. The area of that flow is 22,860 hectares, even though the eruption didn't last more than ten days.[36]

During that time, the crater at the top emitted only thick vapors, sand and ashes.

Thanks to the great kindness of Signor Ragusa, a member of the Alpine Club and the proprietor of the Grand Hotel, we made the ascent of this volcano with extreme facility, an ascent somewhat tiring but in no way perilous.

A train took us first to Nicolosi, through fields and gardens full of trees growing in the pulverized lava. From time to time we traversed some enormous flows, cut by the gash of the road, and everywhere the ground is black.

After three hours of travel and easy climbing, we arrive at the last village at the foot of Etna, Nicolosi, already situated at 700 meters in altitude and at fourteen kilometers from Catania.

There, we leave the train in exchange for guides, mules, coveralls, woolen stockings and gloves, and we set out again.

It is 4 o'clock in the afternoon. The burning sun of oriental lands falls upon this strange land, heating and burning it.

The animals move slowly, with weighed-down steps, in the dust that rises around them like a cloud. The last one, which carries the bundles and provisions, stops at every moment, seemingly saddened by the necessity to retrace, once again, this useless and painful trip.

Around us now are vines, vines planted in the lava, some young, others old. Then here is a moor, a moor of lava covered with flowering gorse, a golden moor; then we cross the enormous flow of 1882; and we stand astounded in front of this immense river, black and motionless, before this boiling and petrified river, come from up there, from the summit, which is smoking, so far off, so far off, about twenty kilometers distant. It has followed valleys, rounded peaks, traversed plains, this river; and here it is now, near us, halted suddenly in its course when its source of fire became exhausted.

We climb, leaving on the left the Monti Rossi, and constantly discovering other mountains, innumerable, which the guides call the sons of Etna, grown up around the monster, which thus wears a necklace of volcanos. There are about three hundred and fifty, these black children of the grandsire, and many among them attain the size of Vesuvius.

Now we are crossing a thin wood still growing in the lava, and suddenly the wind rises up. It is at first a brusque and violent puff, followed by a moment of calm, then a furious squall, scarcely interrupted, which raises and carries off a thick wave of dust.

We stop behind a wall of lava in order to wait, and we remain there until nightfall. Finally we had to set out again, even though the storm was continuing.

And, little by little, the cold grips us, that penetrating mountain cold, which freezes the blood and paralyzes the limbs. It seems hidden, waiting in ambush in the wind; it stings the eyes and eats the skin with its icy bite. We go on, wrapped in our coveralls, entirely in white like the Arabs, gloves on our hands, our heads hooded, allowing our mules, who follow one another, to walk on and stumble along the rugged and dark trail.

Here finally is the Casa del Bosco, a sort of cabin where five or six wood-cutters live. The guide declares that it is impossible to go further in this storm, and we ask for hospitality for the night. The men get up, light the fire and give us two thin straw mattresses, which seem to contain nothing but fleas. The entire cabin shudders and trembles beneath the shocks of the tempest, and the air passes furiously through the disjointed roof-tiles.

We will not see the sunrise from the top of the mountain.

After a few hours of rest without sleep, we go on our way. Daylight has arrived and the wind has calmed down.

Around us now stretches a black land with small valleys, gently rising towards the region of snow which shines blindingly at the base of the last cone, 300 meters high.

Although the sun rises in the midst of an entirely blue sky, the cold, the cruel cold of the great summits, numbs the fingers and burns the skin. Our mules, one behind the other, slowly follow the tortuous path, which twists around all the fantastic shapes in the lava.

Here is the first plain of snow. We avoid it by a detour. But another soon follows it, which must be traversed in a

straight line. The animals hesitate, test it with their hooves, advance carefully. Suddenly I have the abrupt sensation of being swallowed by the ground. The two front legs of my mule, piercing the crust that supported them, have sunk him up to his breast. The animal struggles, distracted, rises up, sinks down again with his four legs, rises up again, only to fall back again.

The others do the same. We have to jump down, calm them, help them, drag them out. At every moment, they plunge up to their bellies into this white and cold foam, which our feet also penetrate now and then up to our knees. Between these passages of snow, which fill up the small valleys, we find again the lava, great plains of lava similar to immense fields of black velvet, brilliant under the sun with as much glare as the snow itself. It is the *deserted region*, the dead region, which seems in mourning, all white and all black, blinding, horrible and splendid, unforgettable.

After four hours of progress and effort, we reach the Casa Inglese, a small stone house, surrounded by ice, almost buried under the snow at the base of the last cone which rises behind, enormous and perfectly straight, crowned with smoke.

It is here that you usually spend the night, on straw, in order to go and see the sunrise from the crater's edge. We leave the mules there and start to climb this frightful wall of hardened cinders, which gives way under foot, where we cannot cling or catch hold on to anything, where we fall back one step out of three. We go on, panting, puffing, thrusting our iron-shod sticks into the soft ground, stopping at every moment.

When we stop we have to plant the sticks between our legs in order not to slide back down again, for the slope is so steep that you cannot even remain seated.

We needed about an hour to climb those 300 meters. For some time already, sulphurous vapors were seizing our throats. We had noticed, sometimes on the right, sometimes on the left, huge jets of smoke escaping from cracks

in the ground; we placed our hands on big burning stones. Finally we reached a narrow platform. Before us, a thick cloud slowly rises, like a white curtain, coming out of the earth. We again advance a few steps, covering our noses and mouths in order not to be suffocated by the sulphur, and suddenly, at our feet, a prodigious, a frightful chasm opens up, measuring about five kilometers in circumference. We scarcely discern, through the suffocating vapors, the other edge of this monstrous hole, 1500 meters in width, whose straight wall sinks down towards the mysterious and terrible region of fire.

The beast is calm. It slumbers at the bottom, at the very bottom. Only the heavy smoke escapes from the prodigious chimney, 3312 meters high.

Round about us it is even stranger. All Sicily is hidden by haze that stops at the edge of the coasts, veiling the earth only, so that we are in the midst of the sky, in the middle of the sea, above the clouds, so high, so high, that the Mediterranean, extending everywhere as far as the eye can see, also resembles blue sky. Azur thus envelopes us on all sides. We are standing on an astonishing mountain, emerged from the clouds and bathed in the heavens that stretch above our heads, beneath our feet, everywhere.

But, little by little, the clouds spread over the island rise around us, soon enclosing the immense volcano in the middle of a circle of clouds, in an abyss of clouds. We are now, in our turn, at the bottom of an entirely white crater, from which we see only the blue firmament up above, while gazing in the air.

On other days, they say that the spectacle is entirely different.

We await the sunrise, which appears behind the hills of Calabria. They cast their shadows far and wide over the sea, up to the foot of Etna, whose silhouette — dark and enormous — covers all of Sicily with its immense triangle, which disappears as the sun ascends into the sky. Then we discern a panorama of more than 400 kilometers in diameter and 1300 in circumference, with Italy to the north along with the Aeolian Islands, whose two volcanos seem to greet their father; then, way to the south, Malta, scarcely visible. In the Sicilian ports, the ships resemble insects on the sea.

Alexandre Dumas *père* has written a very pleasing and very enthusiastic description of this.[37]

We head back down the steep cone of the crater, as much on our backs as on our feet, and we soon enter the thick belt of clouds that envelopes the top of the mountain. After an hour's walk through the haze, we have at last passed through it and we find, under our feet, the indented and green island, with its gulfs, its capes, its towns and the great sea, so very blue, that encloses it.

🦅

After we returned to Catania, we set out the next day for Syracuse.

It is with this small town, singular and charming, that one should end a trip to Sicily. It was as famous as the largest cities; its tyrants had reigns as celebrated as that of Nero; it produced a wine made famous by the poets; it has, on the edge of the gulf which it dominates, a very small river, the Anapo, where papyrus grows, the secret guardian of thought; and it encloses within its walls one of the most beautiful Venus statues in the world.

Some people cross continents to go on a pilgrimage to some miraculous statue — as for me, I have brought my devotions to the Venus of Syracuse!

In a traveler's album, I had seen the photograph of that sublime marble female, and I fell in love with her, as one falls in love with a woman. It was she, perhaps, who made up my mind to undertake this voyage; I spoke about her and I dreamt about her at every moment, before I saw her.

But we arrive too late to enter the museum, entrusted to the care of the learned Professor Francesco Saverio Cavallari — a modern Empedocles who once descended into the crater of Etna to drink a cup of coffee.[38]

I therefore had to traverse the town built on the small island of Ortygia and separated from the land by three enclosures, between which three arms of the sea pass. The town is small, pretty, seated on the edge of the gulf, with gardens and promenades descending down to the waves.

Then we go on to the Latomias, immense excavations open to the sky, which were first stone quarries and afterwards became prisons where were confined for eight months, after the defeat of Nicias, the captured Athenians, tortured

by hunger, thirst, the horrible heat of that cauldron, and the teeming mire in which they suffered.[39]

In one of these, the Latomia of Paradise, you notice, at the rear of a grotto, a strange opening called the Ear of

Dionysius. It is said that he came to the rim of that opening to listen to the moanings of its victims. There are also other versions. Certain ingenious scholars claim that this grotto, set in communication with the theater, served as an underground hall for the performances and furnished it with the echo of its prodigious sonority — for the slightest sounds there take on a surprising resonance.

The most curious of the Latomias is surely that of the Capuchins, a vast and deep garden divided up by vaults, arches, enormous rocks and enclosed by white cliffs.

A little further, we visit the catacombs, which extend over 200 hectares, and where Signor Cavallari discovered one of the most beautiful Early Christian sarcophagi known.[40]

And then we return to the humble hotel that rises above the sea, and we stay up late to reflect, while looking at the red and blue lights of a ship at anchor.

As soon as morning came, since our visit had been announced, they open for us the doors of the charming little palace which holds the collections and the works of art of the city. Upon entering the museum, I saw her, the *Venus of Syracuse*, at the rear of a hall, and as beautiful as I had imagined her to be.

She has no head, an arm is missing; but never has the human form appeared to me more admirable and more suggestive.

It is not the poeticized woman, the idealized woman, the divine or majestic woman, like the Venus de Milo, it is woman as she is, such as we love, such as we desire, such as we want to embrace.

She is corpulent, with a pronounced bosom, strong hips, the legs slightly heavy — a carnal Venus, whom you imagine lying down when seeing her standing. Her lowered arm hides her breasts. With the other hand she lifts a drapery with which she covers, with a delightful gesture, the most mysterious charms. The entire body is made, conceived, adapted for this movement — all the lines concentrate on it, all thought goes there. This simple and natural gesture — full of modesty and immodesty, which hides and reveals, veils and uncovers, lures and conceals — seems to define the whole attitude of mind of women on earth.

And the marble is full of life. You would like to touch it, with the expectation that it will yield to the hand, like flesh. The back, especially, is inexpressibly animated and beautiful. It is displayed with all its charm, that sinuous and fleshy line of the female back, which runs from the nape of the neck to the heels, and which shows — in the contour of the shoulders, in the decreasing roundness of the thighs, and in the slight curve of the thinning calf down to the ankles — all the modulations of human gracefulness. A work of art is only superior if it is, at the same time, a symbol and the exact expression of a reality. The *Venus of Syracuse* is a woman, and it is also the symbol of the flesh.

In front of the head of *La Gioconda* — the *Mona Lisa* — you feel yourself beset by I-know-not-what enervating and mystical temptation of love. There are also some living women whose eyes communicate to us that dream of unrealizable and mysterious tenderness. We seek in them something else behind what is, because they appear to contain and express a little of the ungraspable ideal. We pursue it without ever attaining it, behind all the surprises of beauty, which seem to contain some thought: in the infiniteness of the gaze, which is only a nuance of the iris; in the charm of the smile due to the fold of the lip and a flash of enamel; in the grace of the movement born by chance and the harmony of forms.

Thus the poets, powerless graspers after stars, have always been tormented by the thirst for mystical love. The natural exaltation of a poetic soul, inflamed by artistic excitement, moves these elite beings to imagine a sort of hazy love, desperately tender, ecstatic, never satisfied, sensual without being carnal, so delicate that a mere nothing causes it to disappear — unrealizable and superhuman. And these poets are, perhaps, the only men who have never loved a woman, a real woman of flesh and bones with her womanly qualities, her womanly faults, her limited and charming womanly mind, her womanly nerves and her disquieting femininity.

Every creature who inflames the poet's dream is the symbol of a being, mysterious but magical: the being of whom they sing, those singers of illusions. It is this living being they adore, something like a painted statue, an image of a god the people kneel before. Where is this god? Who is this god? In what part of heaven lives the Unknown they have all idolized, those fools, from the first dreamer to the last? As soon as they touch a hand that responds to their pressure, their souls take flight in an invisible dream, far from carnal reality.

The woman they clasp they transform, perfect and disfigure with their poetic art. Those aren't her lips they kiss, they are the lips of dreams. It isn't in the depths of her blue or black eyes that their excited gaze loses itself, it is in something unknown and unknowable! Their mistress's eye is only a pane of glass through which they try to see the paradise of ideal love.

But if some disquieting women can give this singular illusion to our souls, others only cause the impetuous love, from which our race arises, to quicken in our veins.

The *Venus of Syracuse* is the perfect expression of that powerful beauty, healthy and simple. This admirable torso, in Parian marble, is, they say, the Callipygian Venus described by Athenaeus and Lampridedius, which was given by Heliogabalus to the Syracusians.[41]

She has no head! What of that? The symbol has become more complete. It is a woman's body, which expresses all the real poetry of the caress.

Schopenhauer has said that Nature, wanting to perpetuate the species, has made of reproduction a snare.[42]

This marble form, seen in Syracuse, is indeed the human snare divined by the ancient artist: the woman who hides and reveals the maddening mystery of life.

Is it a snare? Too bad! It invites the mouth, it attracts the hand, it offers to kisses the palpable reality of wonderful flesh, of elastic and white flesh, round and firm and delightful under the embrace.

She is divine, not because she expresses a thought, but only because she is beautiful.

And one thinks, while admiring her, of the bronze ram of Syracuse, the most beautiful object in the museum of Palermo, which also seems to contain all the animalism of the world.[43] The powerful beast is lying down, the body over its hooves and its head turned to the left. And that animal's head seems like a god's head, a bestial god, impure and superb. The forehead is broad and frizzled, the eyes widely set, the nose protruding, long, strong and flat, with a prodigiously brutal expression. The horns, thrown back, fall, twist and turn, spreading their sharp points under thin ears, which themselves resemble two horns. And the beast's gaze

penetrates you — stupid, disturbing and hard. You feel in the presence of a wild animal when approaching this bronze.

Of what temper, then, were the two marvellous artists who thus formulated, under two such different aspects, the simple beauty of a living creature?

There, now, are the only two statues that have left me with the burning desire to see them again, as if they were alive.

At the moment of leaving, I give that marble rump one last glance from the doorway — that glance you toss to women you have loved upon leaving them — and I immediately climb aboard a boat to go and greet — a writer's duty — the papyrii of the Anapo.

We cross the gulf from one side to the other and we espy, on the flat and bare shore, the mouth of a very small river, almost a stream, which the boat enters. The current is strong and difficult to move against. Sometimes they row, sometimes they use the boat-hook to glide over the water, which flows rapidly between two banks covered with yellow flowers, small, bright — two banks of gold.

Here are reeds, which we bruise slightly while passing — bending and rising again, their roots in the water — blue irises of a deep blue, on which flutter innumerable dragonflies with wings of glass, pearl-like and quivering, as large as humming-birds. Now, on the two embankments, which imprison us, giant thistles and enormous convolvulus grow, clasping together the plants of the land and the reeds of the stream.

Beneath us, at the bottom of the water, is a forest of large undulating grasses which stir, float and seem to swim in the current that agitates them.

Then the Anapo separates from the antique Cyane, its tributary. We keep going between the banks, propelled by the long pole. The stream winds, affording charming viewpoints, flowery and delightful perspectives. Finally an island appears, full of strange bushes. The frail and triangular stalks, nine to twelve feet high, carry at their tops round clumps of

green thread — long, thin and supple like hair. You would think they were human heads turned into plants, thrown into the sacred water of the spring by one of the pagan gods who lived there in days gone by. It is the antique papyrus.

The peasants, moreover, call this reed *parruca* ("wig"). Here are others further on, an entire forest. They quiver, murmur, bend, entangle their hairy heads, jostle one another and seem to speak of things unknown and far off.

Is it not strange that the venerable bush, which brought us the thoughts of the dead, which was the guardian of human genius, should have, on its tiny body of a shrub, a big mane, thick and floating, in the same way as the poets? We return to Syracuse while the sun sets and we notice in the harbor a steamer, just arriving, which, this very evening, will carry us towards Africa.

※ ※ ※

NOTES

"La Sicile" *(Sicily)* first appeared in installments in *Le Figaro* and *Gil Blas* between May 1885 and January 1886.; it was published integrally in *La nouvelle revue* in November 1886. Maupassant included it as one chapter of *La vie errante (The Wandering Life)*, published in Paris in 1890 by Paul Ollendorff. The first English translations were included in multi-volume editions of Maupassant's work: *The Life Works of Henri René Guy de Maupassant*, trans. Paul Bourget (London and New York: M. Walter Dunne, 1903), vol. 12; and *The Works of Guy de Maupassant*, trans. Albert M.C. McMaster et al. (New York: Classic Publishing Co., c. 1911), vol. 3. It appeared separately as *The Wandering Life, and Short Stories*, trans. and ed. Alfred de Sumichrest et al. (New York: Pearson, 1910). These translations are frequently inaccurate and incomplete in small ways, although they have been occasionally helpful to me for choice of words and turns of phrase. They all lack introductions and notes.

1. A guidebook of 1891, (Luigi Filippo Bolaffio, *Guida di Palermo e suoi dintorni*, Milan: Fratelli Treves, 1891, p. 2) lists the population of Palermo at about 300,000.

2. The painted carts developed in Sicily from the early nineteenth century on. Intended for the transport of merchandise, the carts were decorated to attract buyers. The imagery on their side and rear panels, at first religious in content, gradually adopted themes and the painted style found in playbills and posters prepared for the popular Sicilian theater and, especially, for the contemporary puppet-shows. Scenes related to Charlemagne and the battles of the Normans against the Saracens were frequent, although many other subjects appeared (including the Crusades and the battles of Napoleon, as mentioned by Maupassant). These carts can still be seen on Sicilian streets today, serving the tourist industry. See Marcella Croce, *Pupi, carretti, contastorie: l'epica cavalleresca nelle tradizioni popolari siciliane* (Palermo: D. Flaccovio, 1999), pp. 99ff.

3. This intersection, called Quattro Canti, is at the juncture of the Corso Vittorio Emanuele (east–west) and the Via Maqueda (north–south).

4. On the Palatine Chapel, see William Tronzo, *The Cultures of His Kingdom: Roger II and the Cappella Palatina in Palermo* (Princeton: Princeton University Press, 1997).

5. This scene was in fact invented by the mosaicist Rosario Riolo in the mid-nineteenth century. See Tronzo, *Cultures*, p. 55 and fig. 14. Pierre Puvis de Chavannes (1824–98) was a contemporary French muralist.

6. The popular name given to the church of St. Mary's of the Admiral. For its decoration, see Ernst Kitzinger, *The Mosaics of St. Mary's of the Admiral in Palermo* (Washington, DC: Dumbarton Oaks, 1991).

7. Wagner finished *Parsifal* while staying in Palermo (November 1881–March 1882); the final act (Act III) was completed at the Hotel des Palmes (Grande Albergo e delle Palme, Via Roma) on 13 January 1882 (Ernest Newman, *The Wagner Operas*, New York: Harper & Row, 1949, 2:666). The opera had its premiere at Bayreuth on 22 July of that year; Wagner died in Venice on 13 February 1883.

8. In his last years Wagner could not compose unless in the presence of certain scents. See Ernest Newman, *Wagner as Man & Artist*, London and Toronto: J.M. Dent & Sons, 1914, p. 127.

9. Members of the clergy and wealthy citizens were buried in the catacombs of the Convento dei Cappuccini (in Via Cappucini, in the western suburbs) until 1881; tours are still conducted here, where about 8,000 bodies are preserved. A photograph of the cadavers is published in Jacques Réda, ed., *Album Maupassant* (Paris: Gallimard, 1987), p. 208, fig. 277.

10. Villa Tasca is located in the southwestern suburbs, near Corso Calatafimi.

11. Originally built in the twelfth century as a fortified monastery on Monte Cuccio by King William II.

12. Emilio Pallavicini (1823–1901), general and later senator, who arrived in Palermo in 1885 and suppressed the brigands.

13. Fra Diavolo was the assumed name of Michele Pezza (1771–1806), an Italian bandit and soldier who fought in the service of the king of Naples against the French invasion of the kingdom in 1799. He was captured and hung by the French in 1806.

14. On the architecture of Monreale Cathedral, see Wolfgang Krönig, *Il duomo di Monreale* (Palermo: S.F. Flaccovio, 1965).

15. On the mosaics, see Ernst Kitzinger, *The Mosaics of Monreale* (Palermo: S.F. Flaccovio, 1960).

16. Actually, almost 8,000 square meters.

17. On the cloister, see Roberto Salvini, *Il chiostro di Monreale e la scultura romanica in Sicilia* (Palermo: S.F. Flaccovio, 1962).

18. From "A L'Arc de Triomphe," VI (*Les Voix Intérieures*, IV). The stanza reads:

> Athène est triste, et cache au front du Parthénon
> Les traces de l'Anglais et celles du canon,
>   Et, pleurant ses tours mutilées,
> Rêve à l'artiste grec qui versa de sa main
> Quelque chose de beau comme un sourire humain
>   Sur le profil des propylées!

19. For a good illustration, see *Enciclopedia italiana di scienze, lettere ed arti* (Rome: Istituto della Enciclopedia italiana, 1935), vol. 36, pl. XV, top.

20. See above, n. 11.

21. On the temple of Segesta, which Maupassant gradually leads the reader to in the following paragraphs, see R. Ross Holloway, *The Archaeology of Ancient Sicily* (London and New York: Routledge, 1991), pp. 119–20, figs. 149, 150.

22. On the theater of Segesta, see Holloway, *Archaeology*, pp. 153, 154, fig. 201.

23. On the ruins of Selinunte, see Holloway, *Archaeology*, index, p. 210 (s.v. "Selinus").

24. On the temples of Agrigento, see Holloway, *Archaeology*, index, p. 203 (s.v. "Acragas").

25. There is confusion in the ancient sources concerning which Temple of Juno Lacinia contained Zeuxis' painting and whence came the five beautiful virgins who served as models for Juno (Hera). According to Pliny the Elder, it was at Acragas (Agrigento), but Cicero and Dionysios of Halikarnassos placed it at Croton in southern Italy. See J.J. Pollitt, *The Art of Greece, 1400–31 B.C.*, Englewood Cliffs: Prentice-Hall, 1965, pp. 155–56.

26. See Holloway, *Archaeology*, pp. 116–17, figs. 144, 145.

27. See Holloway, *Archaeology*, pp. 61, 115, 118–19, fig. 148.

28. See Holloway, *Archaeology*, pp. 61, 83, 117–19, figs. 146, 147.

29. In the nineteenth century Sicily possessed a near world monopoly on sulphur production, supported by cheap child labor, which deeply disturbed Maupassant. See M.I. Finley, Denis Mack Smith and Christopher Duggan, *A History of Sicily* (London: Chatto & Windus, 1986), pp. 161, 193.

30. The island of Vulcano is one of the Aeolian Islands, located off the northeast coast of Sicily.

31. Actually 183 BCE.

32. Originally erected in the Hellenistic period, it was almost entirely rebuilt under the Romans. On the theater in Taormina, see Holloway, *Archaeology*, p. 154.

33. Goethe in 1787 exclaimed (referring to the view from the topmost seats): "Never did any audience, in any theater, have before it such a spectacle" (*Italian Journey*, trans. Robert R. Heitner, New York: Suhrkamp, 1989, p. 236).

34. Actually, 474. Pindar's description is found in his Pythian Ode I. The Greek poet described Etna's usual volcanic activity, not a major eruption.

35. The Sicans were one of three indigenous peoples whom the Greeks encountered when they began colonizing Sicily in the eighth century BCE; the others were the Sicels and the Elymians. See L. Bernabò Brea, *Sicily before the Greeks,* trans. C.M. Preston and L. Guido (London: Thames & Hudson, 1957).

36. A list of eruptions is published in David K. Chester et al., *Mount Etna: The Anatomy of a Volcano* (Stanford: Stanford University Press, 1985), pp. 350–52 (Table 9.4). There are some discrepancies between this list and Maupassant's account.

37. Alexandre Dumas *père, Impressions de voyage. Le spéronare,* new ed. (Paris: Michel Lévy Frères, 1873), 1:224–25.

38. Empedocles, the Greek philosopher (5th c. BCE) was said to have leapt into the crater of Etna. Matthew Arnold's long poem, "Empedocles on Etna" (written 1849–52), concludes with the suicide leap.

39. Thucydides, *The Peloponnesian War* 7.86–87.

40. The *Sarcophagus of Adelfia* (Syracuse, Museo Archeologico Regionale Paolo Orsi). See Guido Libertini, *Il Regio Museo Archeologico di Siracusa* (Rome: La Libreria dello Stato, 1929), pp.171–72 (illus. on p. 170).

41. The *Venus of Syracuse* (also known as the *Landolina Venus*; Museo Archeologico Regionale Paolo Orsi) is in the pose of the *Capitoline* or *Medici Venus.* See Francis Haskell and Nicholas Penny, *Taste and the Antique: The Lure of Classical Sculpture, 1500–1900* (New Haven and London: Yale University Press, 1981), pp. 318–20, no. 84, fig. 169, pp. 325–28, no. 88, fig. 173.

Maupassant had apparently been informed that the statue was the *Callipygian Venus,* since a shrine to that goddess had recently been discovered on Sicily. See Libertini, *Il Regio Museo,* p. 167. However, that Venus is a figure in an entirely different pose, perhaps meant to be viewed primarily from the rear. See *ibid.,* pp. 316–18, no. 83, figs. 168 and 21.

The left hand of the *Venus of Syracuse* holds drapery which streams downward into space to left and right in a graceful and original way; open in the front, it seems wind-blown. The presence of the dolphin (suggesting the sea; the motif also found in the *Medici Venus*) identifies the figure as a Venus Anadyomene, covering herself after coming ashore on Cyprus. The sculpture, of Parian marble, was discovered on the outskirts of Syracuse in 1804. It is a replica (second or first century BCE) of a very famous Hellenistic original (not before the third century BCE). For a cogent discussion, see Libertini, *Il Regio Museo*, pp. 166–68.

42. See Bryan Magee, *The Philosophy of Schopenhauer*, rev. ed. (Oxford and New York: Clarendon Press and Oxford University Press, 1997), pp. 216ff.

43. The Bronze Ram of Syracuse (Palermo, Museo Archeologico Regionale) is dated to the beginning of the third century BCE. See Sabatino Moscati and Carmela Angela Di Stefano, *Palermo: Museo archeologico*, Palermo: Edizioni Novecento, 1991, pp. 83–84. Its companion was destroyed at the end of the eighteenth century.

BIBLIOGRAPHY

Bibliographical Guide

Olivastri, Valentina. *Sicily.* World Bibliographical Series, vol. 213. Oxford, Santa Barbara, Denver: Clio Press, 1998. This lists books on all aspects of Sicily through the ages.

History

Finley, M.I., Dennis Mack Smith and Christopher Duggan. *A History of Sicily.* London: Chatto & Windus, 1986. The classic survey of the entire, complex history of the island.

Maupassant's artistic interests while he was in Sicily focused on ancient Greek and Norman–Byzantine art and architecture. For these topics see:

The Greeks in Sicily

Boardman, John. *The Greeks Overseas: Their Early Colonies and Trade.* London: Thames & Hudson, 1980.

Fischer-Hansen, Tobias. *Ancient Sicily.* Copenhagen: Museum Tusculanum Press, Collegium Hyperboreum, 1995.

Guido, Margaret. *Sicily: An Archaeological Guide.* London: Faber & Faber, 1977.

Holloway, R. Ross. *The Archaeology of Sicily.* London and New York: Routledge, 1991.

Pugliese Carratelli, Giovanni, ed. *The Western Greeks: Classical Civilization in the Western Mediterranean*. London: Thames & Hudson, 1996.

The Normans in Sicily

Borsook, Eve. *Messages in Mosaic: The Royal Programmes of Norman Sicily, 1130–1187*. Oxford and New York: Clarendon Press and Oxford University Press, 1990.

Capitani, Ovidio, Giuseppe Galasso and Roberto Salvini. *The Normans in Sicily and Southern Italy*. Oxford: Oxford University Press, 1977.

Demus, Otto. *The Mosaics of Norman Sicily*. London: Routledge & Kegan Paul, 1949.

Matthew, Donald. *The Norman Kingdom of Sicily*. Cambridge: Cambridge University Press, 1992.

Norwich, John Julius. *The Normans in Sicily*. London: Penguin Books, 1967, 1970.

Travel Memoirs and Descriptions

Bradford, Ernle. *The Wind off the Island*. London: Grafton Books, 1988.

Bufalino, Gesualdo, ed. *Cento Sicilie: Testimonianze per un ritratto*. Scandicci: La Nuova Italia Editrice, 1993. Anthology.

Cronin, Vincent. *The Golden Honeycomb: A Sicilian Quest*. Rev. ed., London: Harvill, 1992. First edition, 1954.

Dumas *père*, Alexandre. *Le Spéronare*. Paris: Dumont, 1842. Later editions: *Impressions de voyage. Le Spéronare*.

Durrell, Lawrence. *Sicilian Carousel*. New York: Viking, 1977.

Fallowell, Duncan. *To Noto, or London to Sicily in a Ford*. London: Bloomsbury Publishing, 1991.

Goethe, Johann Wolfgang von. *Die italienische Reise (The Italian Journey, 1786–88)*. Many translations.

Knight, Richard Payne. *Expedition into Sicily*. Ed. by Claudia Stumpf. London: British Museum Publications, 1986.

Levi, Carlo. *Words Are Stones: Impressions of Sicily*. Trans. by Angus Davidson, London: Victor Golllancz, 1959.

Simeti, Mary Taylor. *On Persephone's Island*. New York: Vintage Books, 1995. First edition, 1986.

ITALICA HISTORICAL TRAVEL GUIDES

FORTHCOMING

Pierre Gilles' Constantinople, edited by Kimberly Byrd

ALREADY PUBLISHED

Guide to the Holy Land, by Theoderich of Würzburg

In Old Paris, edited by Robert W. Berger

Lisbon in the Renaissance, by Damião de Góis

The Marvels of Rome, Mirabilia Urbis Romae

Naples: An Early Guide, by Enrico Bacco et al.

Norman London, by William Fitz Stephen

Paris: An Electronic Tour of the Old City,
edited by Robert W. Berger

The Pilgrim's Guide to Santiago de Compostela,
by William Melczer

The Road to Compostela for Macintosh & Windows

Travels in the Middle Ages:
The Itinerary of Benjamin of Tudela

This Book Was Completed on August 13, 2007 at
Italica Press, New York, New York. It
Was Set in Giovanni and Printed
on 60-lb Natural Paper
by BookMobile,
St. Paul, MN
U. S. A.